Grace Thus Far

A Journey of Hope and Healing

Updated Edition
© 2010

By Ginger Millermon

To Joel

I'm so glad we weathered the storm together.
Thank you for all your encouragement and support.

You're my best. I love you.

Forward

This is the story of Jarrott Millermon, a premature infant, and his struggle to remain on this side of eternity. As one of many physicians involved in his care I was familiar with Jarrott's medical history, but I really didn't know the whole story until I read this book. These pages opened my eyes beyond the physician's narrowly focused vision to really see what went on in Jarrott's family and especially in the heart of his mother, Ginger, during the long months he battled for life.

Jarrott was subject to state-of-the-art technology in the attempt to save him, but Ginger revealed the real struggle which was broader and deeper than most of us see on the surface. Ginger, an enviably multitalented song-writer and singer, kept a journal during this time allowing accurate rendition of her thoughts and emotions in real time, unclouded by the intervening years. I was amazed at the level of her understanding and ability to deal with the difficulties of her critically ill infant.

At the same time, she kept a Biblical perspective and in this book shared the Scripture passages that helped her understand and deal with a seemingly unending series of troubling events.

Adventure seems to accompany the Millermons wherever they go. Ginger related the real adventure of Jarrott's story—from the stark hospital rooms to the warmth and support of a gathered family. A genuine roller coaster, I laughed out loud then choked back tears. Ginger chronicles the joys, triumphs and trials undergirded by faith in Christ. This book will encourage you to persevere, to "run with endurance the race that is set before us" (Heb 12:1).

—David Pacini, MD, FAAP

"For I know the plans I have for you," declares the Lord, "plans to prosper you and not to harm you, plans to give you a hope and a future."

—Jeremiah 29:11

Part I

Chapter One

____

August 1996

ON TUESDAY, AUGUST 6, 1996, my life changed forever.

My idyllic days as a young mother and youth pastor's wife in our quaint little Colorado town were about to be irreparably disrupted. Up to this point, my life hadn't necessarily been perfect or always easy, but it certainly hadn't been tragic. I'm so glad I didn't have even a glimpse of the winding, rocky road that lay ahead for our family. The valleys would be deep and the rivers raging. Despair, doubt, and discouragement lurked right around our corner. Yet as I look back, I can see God's sufficient and constant grace.

But let me back up a bit. Before the unimaginable trials and anguish set in, we were having a normal summer retreat with some of the teenagers in our youth group. My handsome and energetic husband, Joel, served as a youth pastor in a little Bible church in a tiny coalmining town called Paonia. A lean, tall former college basketball player, Joel was still definitely a kid at heart and was always challenging the local boys to a rousing game of "pick up" at the church gym. Often in the middle of a heated, sweaty game, he'd call time out and stop the game for some devotions. It was proving to be an effective way to reach many of the hardened kids in our town. Joel had such a heart for that community, as it was his hometown and he knew the challenges and temptations facing the teens. I was helping him in his ministry, discipling and teaching the teenage girls and loving the life we had with our church family.

I was especially enjoying our eighteen-month-old daughter, McKenzie. She was the light of our life with her snappy brown eyes and Shirley Temple curls. Although not yet two, she had an amazing vocabulary and loved entertaining us with her hilarious comments. When she was a little confused about something we'd tell her, she'd cock her head to one side and ask, "What say?" She filled our days with laughter and had her daddy wrapped around her little finger. We were also thrilled to be expecting our second child in three months. Since we had our precious girl, I was really hoping for a boy.

As we worked with our youth group, we were so excited and pleased to see some of the teens truly growing in the Lord and serious about their walk with Him. We decided to take about ten of them—the ones who were showing some spiritual leadership and maturity—for a three-day retreat up into the mountains. We planned a packed weekend of devotions, Bible training, and hiking in the rugged foothills of the Spanish Peaks. We brought along another experienced mom, my good friend, Lynn, to help with cooking, which allowed me to stay off of my feet as much as possible. I had undergone preterm labor and bed rest with McKenzie and we were trying to prevent going through that again. Lynn, with her boisterous laugh, radiated fun and helped me keep up with the teens' crazy schedules and unending appetites.

Of course, I couldn't know that Joel and the teenagers

would get caught in a lightning storm five miles up the mountain. They were drenched to the bone in freezing rain as lightning struck the shale all around them. One of the boys, a lanky teen named Bob, had pulled his jacket up over his head and exposed his lower back to the freezing sleet, causing his body temperature to lower dangerously. When Bob began to wander off through the woods and act irrationally, Joel recognized the signs of hypothermia and gathered everyone around to help warm up Bob while two of the boys started down the mountain for help.

Lynn, McKenzie, and I were enjoying a quiet afternoon in the cabin when Lynn's son, Jared, burst into the cabin yelling.

"Bob's got hypothermia. He needs help!" He was so out of breath we could barely understand him.

"What? Jared, that's not funny!" His mom reprimanded him, thinking he was joking.

"Mom, I'm serious. We got caught in a storm and he's not responsive. Pastor Joel sent me to get help. They need paramedics up there."

Lynn and I looked at each other, momentarily at a loss. The canyon had no phones and neither of us had a cell phone that worked.

I was trying to think of the fastest way to get help when I remembered some friends we'd met down the road mentioned they had a phone to call out on. I jumped up and started running for their cabin. Barefoot and very pregnant, my blue eyes huge and my waist-length blond hair streaming behind me, I was a sight to behold, racing as fast as my little legs would take me.

Within the hour, rescue squads arrived and by the time they reached Bob, he was recovering. Shaken up and anxious to return to the warm cabin, we had a sober group of teens that night. It was a scary few hours, but in the end the whole experience brought our youth group closer together as the teens faced the fact that many of the petty things they tended to focus on really didn't matter.

The kids retreat was for three days, and our plan was that Joel would drive the teens the six hours back home and I'd stay at the cabin with McKenzie overnight. Joel would then return the next day for our family vacation. It seemed like a good plan at the time. Until the bat arrived.

Our second day at the cabin we had an unexpected and unwelcome guest. One very furry and fierce-looking little brown bat swooped down from the rafters and chased us around the cabin. The teenagers named our new cabin occupant Clyde and offered it watermelon on a stick while I suggested someone get a gun. There's nothing like a teen's delight at seeing the youth pastor's chubby, pregnant wife crawl under the kitchen table to escape a swooping bat. I had been free entertainment for sure. That *alone* could send any pregnant woman into labor.

But our bat adventure hadn't stopped there.

As I waved goodbye to Joel and the vanload of teens that sunny morning, I thought of all the fun things McKenzie and I would do that day. Throw rocks in the stream. Take a nap. Maybe go for a short walk. Take a nap. Eat lunch. Take a nap. I was feeling like Garfield the Cat by this time in my pregnancy.

After Joel and the kids left, I had a fleeting concern about the bat issue. I figured Clyde was just a one-night thing and he'd leave me alone—at least until Joel got back. Wrong! Late that night as McKenzie slept in her playpen, I sat on the couch reading my Bible. It was so peaceful and quiet. No television, no phone, no email. Just solitude. I loved it.

As the sound of the stream and the book of Psalms lulled me half asleep, Clyde descended from the rafters, diving right

at me for a flyby. I screamed and swung my Bible at him. It
brought a whole new meaning to God's Word being a sword.
To my horror, the bat flew along the floor into McKenzie's
room. I raced—okay, waddled—into her room and threw a
blanket over the top of her playpen. I had no one to call, no
one to rescue me. I did have Joel's 9mm handgun and I
seriously thought about blowing that bat right out of the air.
But what were the chances I'd actually hit him? Slim to none,
I was pretty sure. After a couple of hours, I ended up going to
bed with the covers over my head, chanting "the fervent
prayer of a righteous man availeth much." You couldn't get
more fervent than me at that point.

Fortunately, everything looked better in the morning.
Clyde was gone and McKenzie and I had another fantastic day
together. I felt a twinge of a tightening in my belly here and
there, but nothing profound. Looking back, I suppose balan-
cing barefoot on top of a fence post to hang a hummingbird
feeder in a tree hadn't been the best idea. I never even mentioned that to Joel. Some things, he really didn't need to
know.

That evening as the shadows got long, I put McKenzie to
bed and sat down to wait for Joel. As I lay on the couch
reading my Bible, I suffered a *déjà vu* moment and glanced up
at the rafters. Though uneasy, I knew Joel would be arriving
any time.

I could not believe it when Clyde made an appearance
again and, like some psycho kamikaze, dove right for my face!
I stood to my feet, brandished my Bible over my head and
yelled, "I hate you, Clyde!" What must the neighbors have
thought? Crazy pregnant lady.

By this time he was back to the rafters, hanging. I kept a
wary eye on him and was so glad to hear Joel's tires crunching
on the gravel a few minutes later.

Instead of a kiss, I frantically greeted Joel with, "Clyde's here! He's been swooping at me and chasing me!" I grabbed my husband by the shirtfront and shook him. "You've got to kill him!" What a welcoming sight I must have made for my tired husband.

Like any knight in shining armor, he went on a bat hunt while I cowered in the bedroom. Joel has always been my hero. With expressive chocolate brown eyes that snagged me the first day I met him and usually an ornery grin on his face, he looks unassuming, but he can do a little bit of everything. He climbed to the loft, searched through the rafters, and looked under the beds. No Clyde. I was so disappointed. I wanted the bat dead.

Exhausted from his trip, Joel finally crawled into bed and started to fall asleep while I went to the bathroom to wash up. I slipped off my glasses and washed my face. Just one tiny, dim light bulb hung in the rustic bathroom over a little mirror. I'm virtually blind without my glasses so I got up close to the mirror to make sure I'd washed off all my makeup.

My heart almost stopped dead in its tracks when I saw Clyde hanging underneath that light bulb, mere inches from my face. His eyes bored menacingly into mine. Joel will attest to the fact that the scream reverberating from the bathroom was inhuman.

I shot out of that bathroom like a greased pig out of a rocket. Joel raced to the kitchen and got a hammer. Clyde was going to be stopped once and for all. I crawled under the covers, my heart pounding, while Joel went to war. He grabbed a plastic sack to capture Clyde. He'd decided when Clyde flew into the sack, he'd beat him with the hammer. It sounded like a good plan, yet every time Joel got close, Clyde's evil eyes would open wide and he'd glare at Joel, freaking him out. It didn't help that both of us were now terrified of the bat!

Knowing this could go on for hours, I finally yelled from the safety of the bedroom, "Do I need to come and do it myself?" Ever the quiet, supportive wife.

That was all it took. Joel shook off his bat phobia and made his move. He trapped Clyde in the sack right as the bat flew at him. He slammed it to the floor and as he reached for the hammer, the unthinkable happened: Clyde found a hole in the sack! He scooted out of the hole just as Joel brought the hammer down. I heard a lot of commotion coming from the bathroom, and soon Joel emerged the victor, holding the sack high. He went outside and buried the monster. McKenzie had slept through it all. I certainly rested much better that night.

After all the excitement, I started to feel more and more light contractions and called my doctor's office the next morning to make an appointment for the day we returned home. The tightenings were light and irregular, but still concerning. I spent the last few days of our vacation off my feet and resting. After our bat drama was over, we started to realize how funny the whole situation was. We shared our story the next day with some friends who were staying down the road and they wished they had seen me swinging my "sword" at Clyde. Everyone was relieved I had refrained from using the gun.

As soon as we got home, Joel left to counsel at a teen camp up in the mountains, several hours away. My parents arrived from Kansas for a visit, so my dad, always trying to take care of his little girl, volunteered to drive me the thirty miles to our doctor's office. Soon I was in the examining room, explaining the contractions to my doctor. He'd experienced my early labor with McKenzie and didn't seem overly concerned or surprised. Until he examined me.

"Uh-oh."

It's never a good thing when your doctor says, "Uh-oh."

"What?" I asked, "What's wrong?"

"You're already dilating and the baby is footling breach. He's upside down. That's not good. I need to send you over to the hospital for a sonogram." He snapped off his gloves and reached for the phone.

When he hung up he said, "Okay, head on over to the hospital and they'll be ready for you. I'll come by and check on you there."

Again, I wasn't too worried at this point. I'd been on several months of bed rest with McKenzie and assumed I was in for a couple of long, boring months again. Feeling more bummed out than scared, I grabbed my dad in the waiting room, and we drove to the hospital. Dad knew the wait would be long so he dropped me off for the afternoon and drove back to Paonia.

Before long I was in a maternity room waiting for the technician. She arrived without even a smile or friendly comment and got right to work. I jumped a little as she squeezed the cold jelly onto my stomach to start the sonogram. I was so excited to see this little person, I couldn't stop chattering.

"This baby moves all the time, huh? I can hardly sleep at night and I just can't seem to stop eating! I'm hungry all the time." The technician nodded politely and watched the screen. I leaned my head to the side and tried to catch a glimpse of the picture on the computer screen. I'd promised Joel I wouldn't find out whether we were having a boy or a girl while he was at camp, but I was dying to know. I thought at least I could get a glimpse of the baby. To my slight irritation, the technician moved the screen out of my viewing range. One would think she'd know better than to irritate a pregnant woman! Since I couldn't see the baby, I simply plied her with questions.

"Can you tell what it is? Don't tell me, but can *you* tell?"

She didn't respond and it was several minutes before she looked at me, perplexed.

"Is this your first sonogram?"

"Yes, our insurance wouldn't cover one unless there was a medical need." I was a little confused by her abrupt tone. She seemed pretty uptight and I quickly concluded she had absolutely no sense of humor. I took that as a personal challenge and kept talking to fill the awkward silence.

"I just feel like there are knees and elbows everywhere and I've had the *worst* heartburn…"

"So you're telling me this is your first sonogram?" she interrupted, again.

"Yes." I said slowly. This time I let the silence sit between us.

A couple of minutes passed and I couldn't believe it when she turned to me again and repeated her only question.

"So you've never had a sonogram with this pregnancy?"

Now I took a good long look at her. With her straight brown hair and white lab coat, she was ultra professional. I determined she had to be somewhere in her mid-thirties— which seemed sort of old to me at the time. But I was really thinking she was having some sort of premature short-term memory loss. I answered her again, this time a little louder and slower just in case.

"Yes…this is my first sonogram." A distinctly unpleasant thought occurred to me. "Is the baby okay?" I had the feeling she knew something I didn't.

A heartbeat passed. "Yes, the…the baby is fine."

The feeling grew. "Well…" I said with a nervous laugh. "There's just one in there, right?" I voiced the question that had become a huge family joke as I got larger and larger with the pregnancy.

I will never forget that moment. It was one of those times that stretch out slowly, dreamlike. Similar to the one where you're running in slow motion down the street in your underwear in the middle of a parade.

She turned to me with a look of chagrin, her head shaking back and forth. "I don't think I'm supposed to tell you this, but..." I went numb. "There's definitely two in there."

With a speed beforehand unrecorded for pregnant women, I sat up and grabbed the poor woman's arm. Shaking it, I demanded, "That's a joke, right?" I thought she'd finally been wooed by my cunning charm and found something funny to say. Instead she turned the computer screen toward me for the first time and pointed.

"This is Baby A and this is Baby B."

Baby A and Baby B? What on earth? Sure enough, as I peered at the screen I could see two hearts beating side by side. I relaxed my death grip on the technician's arm and lay back down. Within seconds, I launched back upright on the examining table.

"Well, there's just two in there, right?"

Her answer terrified me. "Honey, I can't tell yet how many are in there."

All of the bizarre things that had happened to me in my life flashed through my mind—like the time I got my dress caught in the locked door as I was leaving for church and I had to shimmy out of it and race to my in-laws in my slip, or the time in high school when I was finally on the date of my dreams with my brother's best friend and I dumped my whole salad in my lap on my white pants, or how about when my dog landed me on crutches during dog obedience class. *We're probably having a litter! Ten, twelve. Who knows? I'm going to be on the front of the* National Enquirer *tomorrow: "Colorado Woman has Twelve Babies!"*

Tears started rolling down my cheeks, pooling in my ears as I waited. Finally, she spoke up. "Okay, I can see everything and there's just two."

I let out a huge sigh. Two was looking easy by now after all the images flitting through my mind in the previous five minutes.

"Well, if there are two, maybe you'd better just tell me what they are. I probably should know."

Her first genuine smile. "They're definitely both boys."

Well, then I *knew* for sure God had a sense of humor, because I was thinking two boys at once was absolutely crazy! Then practicality set in. *We can't be having two boys! We just carpeted the bathroom! Potty training will be a nightmare! Why didn't we just go with the linoleum?*

Things flew into high gear from there—call the doctor, administer medications to stop labor. And I started phoning family. Joel, of course, was first on the list. I got the number to the camp and told the director I needed to speak to Joel right away. I'm sure the hysteria in my voice convinced him to call Joel in from the game he was playing with the teens. I was still in shock and very overwhelmed by the time Joel came to the phone.

"Honey, I'm in the hospital and we're having twins and they're BOYS!" I wailed.

I expected immediate sympathy. Was I ever surprised.

"YES!" he whooped. "Twin boys!"

I heard the phone drop. "Hey, Steve," he hollered to his brother. "We're having twin boys!" He was delirious with joy. Finally, he picked the phone back up.

"Oh, honey," he said, breathless with excitement. "I've always wanted twins."

It was at that moment I realized we should have gone much further in our premarital counseling. This is something I should have known about, fasted, and prayed over. Consulted many counselors and weighed carefully before I married this man. It was certainly too late now. It was also a mighty good thing he was about two hours away because it really was not a good time to be sharing this little morsel of information with me. Suddenly it all became clear. We were having twin boys. And it was all Joel's fault.

…So I will not
Lean on my own understanding
And I know
You'll see me through
If I'll acknowledge you
In all my ways…

Chapter Two

———

August 1996

ONCE THE DOCTOR discovered I was having twins and already dilating at twenty-nine weeks, things flew into action. After my panicked phone call to Joel, he got into the car and started his two-hour drive down the mountain to the hospital. While I waited for him to arrive, I had plenty of time to get overwhelmed. A flurry of activity surrounded me as the doctor and nurses tried to find the quickest way to get me to a larger hospital. The Flight for Life helicopter was called and it looked like I'd be flown to St. Mary's Hospital in Grand Junction. At the last minute the helicopter was called to another emergency, so I was to be transported by ambulance. I was given more medications and was starting to feel groggy by the time they loaded me in for the thirty-mile drive to St. Mary's. Joel arrived just as the ambulance was pulling out and he followed us.

By the time I was settled into the hospital, I had dilated to six centimeters. The doctors were concerned they wouldn't be able to stop labor in time to give me more steroids for the babies' lungs. With the boys trying to come ten weeks early, the threat of underdeveloped lungs and other health issues was high. I don't have too many memories of the next several days, except extreme discomfort.

I was put on magnesium sulfate to stop contractions and the head of my bed was lowered to take all the pressure off my cervix. Every sip of water or anything I ate came right back up, since my head was below my stomach. It was one of the most uncomfortable weeks of my life. I begged more than once to be laid flat in the bed. Delirium, bedpans, ice chips, monitors and frequent blood draws defined the next six days. I had no concept of the gravity of our situation or of the problems we could have if the boys were too early. I wanted to have the babies and be out of my misery. The medications were making me loopy and blurring my vision. I couldn't even make out faces or mumble a sentence without slurring my words.

One morning I was rambling on and on to Joel about how beautiful the river was outside my window. He was quite confused. The only thing outside my third-story window was a roof covered with gravel. My eyes and my brain weren't working right! Joel was still so excited about having twins. He and my mom took turns by my bedside, and Joel slept on a cot in my room. While Mom sat with me, he'd go out and look at minivans because our compact car was not going to hold three car seats. Each good deal he found, he'd call me from his cell phone to tell me all about it. In my medicated state of mind, I'm surprised I didn't tell him to buy the whole car lot. Joel was also trying to keep up with the details of a fundraiser the youth group had planned for weeks. They were selling submarine sandwiches at the local county fair and it was Joel's responsibility to coordinate the whole thing. His older sisters, Kristi and Kathy, and his mom willingly jumped into the role and took over in his absence. He was on the phone with them several times a day trying to answer questions and keep the fundraiser going.

My sixth day into bed rest, IVs and catheters, my contractions finally faded and stopped. The doctors put me on a more comfortable medication and allowed me to sit up in bed. In fact, they moved me out of the labor room and constant monitoring to a regular room on the floor. I was so excited— well, as excited as I could be after the doctor dropped the news I'd be in the hospital for at least the next month. They'd barely stopped labor and they weren't taking any more chances. I'd be a resident on the labor and delivery floor for a month or as long as they could hold off labor.

My mom, who is petite and blond and my very best girlfriend, sat in my hospital room and brainstormed about the best way to take care of McKenzie and how we were going to get ready for two babies. Mom completely saved my sanity. With her servant heart and organizational genius, she was full of ideas on how to make the space work in our little house. McKenzie was still using the crib, so we didn't even have a spot for these little guys. I thought about all my plans to have McKenzie potty trained before the new baby came and have the baby room all ready to go. I was feeling pretty frustrated and helpless that I couldn't do *anything*. On top of that, I hadn't been out of bed for days and I was pleading with my nurses and doctor for bathroom privileges.

"Can't you just take out the catheter and let me at least use the bathroom? I just need to get up a little. *Please?*" I wasn't above begging at this point.

My nurse responded firmly, "You can't be up walking around."

"Just to the bathroom?" It was only a few feet from my bed.

She sighed. "Let me check."

A few minutes later she was back and said the doctor had given permission for the catheter to be removed and bathroom privileges were granted. I was ecstatic!

I still had my IV in for fluids, so I had to use the bathroom more times than I'd planned. On one short trip to the bathroom I even stopped by the window for a moment and looked out at the lush green summer day. I felt guilty about that extra little stop for months. I should have obeyed my doctor...just to the bathroom and back.

It was after lunch when I felt the first familiar tightening. Joel was out buying soda for the fundraiser when I felt the slightest tension across my ever-growing belly. Panic spiraled in me. I did not want to go back on the monitors and magnesium sulfate. I lay as still as I could in my bed, sipping plenty of water, hoping it would go away. Pretty soon it happened again. Just the slightest feeling, but I knew those symptoms well. I pushed the button on my bed for the nurse.

"Yes?" She hustled into the room.

"I'm feeling something again. It's really light, but I'm having little contractions."

"Well, your uterus is probably irritable. That's normal. Do they hurt at all?"

"No, they're just slight tightenings."

"Well, we'll hook you up to the monitor and check it out, but I'm sure you're probably fine." She frowned. "No more getting up for a while."

How did she know? I felt my face flush. "I won't."

The nurse brought in the fetal monitor and pulled the straps around my belly. As she turned the machine on, I felt another swell. This time a little harder.

"Okay, I'm going to let this go for awhile. I'll be back in to check on you and look at the read-out." She made a few notes on my chart and left the room.

I kept my eyes on the monitor as it printed out the activity. I could see a slight bump on the paper corresponding with another little contraction. A moment passed and I felt something all too familiar. This one was not a little irritation. My heart pounded as I saw a huge peak print out on the paper. I reached for the cell phone and the nurses' button at the same time.

Joel picked up right away. "What's going on?"

"Honey, I think you'd better get back here to the hospital. I'm having contractions again."

"How bad? Are they regular?"

"Not yet, but they're getting there. I had a big one. You'd better hurry."

The obstetrician had told us that because one of the boys was footling breech, he wanted to know before I started to dilate again. He'd stressed to us the crisis we'd have on our hands if Baby A reached the birth canal going feet first.

My nurse popped in. "What do you need?"

I pointed to the monitor. There on the read-out was a series of little bumps and a couple large mounds.

"Oh my." She reached for her phone and paged the obstetrician. He arrived right behind Joel.

"How long has this been going on?" Dr. King asked me, his bushy black moustache moving back and forth.

"Not very long. I started to feel some slight contractions about an hour ago, but all of a sudden they've gotten harder. I've had four hard ones."

He checked the cervix and looked solemnly at Joel and me. "Let's call the anesthesiologist."

I was dilated to eight centimeters, and there was no time to waste.

I tried not to panic as my room suddenly swarmed with

nurses. As one of the nurses escorted me one more time to the bathroom she asked gently, "Now, has anyone explained what's going to happen with the C-section?"

I shook my head. I was totally unprepared for how quickly everything was happening. Dr. King had told us it would be an emergency if I started to dilate, but the gravity of the situation still hadn't sunk in with me.

"Well, we're going to get you to the operating room and get you prepped for surgery." She walked me to the bed and helped me lie down. As they pushed my bed out of the room and down the long hall, she continued. "The anesthesiologist will meet us there and will give you an epidural. You won't feel anything from about the chest down." She patted my arm. "They'll take good care of you."

I felt sick to my stomach as nurses and doctors bustled around me in the operating room. Joel had gone to scrub and get into his mask and gown so he could be with me during the surgery. I was relieved to have him back at my side as my body went numb with the anesthesia and epidural. It was the scariest feeling to not be able to feel my lower body. I could move my arms a little, but they were strapped down. I tried to wiggle my toes, but it didn't feel like anything was there.

I was starting to panic when a face popped into view. All I could see was a pair of bright green eyes between a blue mask and cap.

"I'm Ann. I'm the neonatologist and I'm here to take care of your babies." Her voice was compassionate, yet confident.

Comfort flooded my heart as I looked into her kind eyes. I knew my babies were in good hands.

The anesthesiologist stood at the head of my bed watching my vitals as Dr. King performed the Cesarean section. I was slightly amused when Dr. King assured me he was doing the incision so I could still wear a bikini on the beach if I wanted to. Boy, that was really a high priority to me at the moment. I couldn't even imagine getting this pregnant-with-twins body back into swimwear.

Joel was videotaping from a modest angle as they pulled one, then two tiny boys from my belly. I scarcely even got to see the little bits of fuzz on their heads and their miniature fingers as they were whisked by my head for a quick look before Ann took them to get Apgar scores and check them over. The Apgar score would test and rate the boys' color, breathing, pulse, and activity.

Joel and I had brainstormed for weeks and struggled to come up with baby names. Of course we didn't know we were having two, so we thought we'd just need one boy and one girl name. Ironically enough, we'd come up with two boy names and no girl names. We'd been going back and forth between Brennan Joel and Jarrott David. Brennan was a name I'd seen in a book and I loved it. It also worked well with Joel's name. But Jarrott was my maiden name and I had always wanted to name one of our boys Jarrott. So the names were settled ahead of time and little Baby A, who had been causing so many troubles being footling breech, was to be named Brennan Joel. He was born at 4:45 PM on August 6, 1996. He weighed a whopping 2 pounds 14.8 ounces. Jarrott David was two minutes behind him at 4:47. He was a tenth of an ounce bigger at 2 pounds 14.9 ounces.

I smiled up at Joel through my tears. He had his twin boys. I had to think of all the crazy things we'd been through in the few short years we'd been together. From being robbed on vacation and a hurricane on our first and only cruise, to a near-disastrous skiing trip, I was pretty sure this was just the beginning of another big adventure. I thought back almost exactly six years earlier to the day we first met, on another hot August afternoon. Before classes even started my freshman year and Joel's senior year of college, I dropped my books and Joel, ever the gentleman, rushed to help me out. What started out as a fun, laughter-filled friendship soon became the lasting love I'd always dreamed of having.

We never could have imagined back then, as young, idealistic college students, what experiences and trials were in store for us in the days and years ahead. If we had known all that we would go through together, we might have just smiled and walked away while we had the chance. I'm so glad I didn't know.

First Breath
By Ginger Millermon
© *Anothen Music 2002*

...For I am fearfully and wonderfully made
Fashioned by God's hand
And my days were written in His book
Long before time began...

Chapter Three

─────

August 1996

THE FIRST SEVERAL days after the boys' birth are still very vague to me. I was recovering from my C-section and experienced a tremendous amount of pain to get out of bed. The morning after they were born I was pushed into the neonatal nursery in my wheelchair and parked between their tiny beds underneath the warmers. I'd been on so many medications leading up to the delivery, I still hadn't quite adjusted to the fact that there were two of them. It didn't seem real to me. To be honest, I didn't feel any distinctive mothering urges when I first saw them. I was overwhelmed and numb. I couldn't believe they were both mine. They were so little, hooked up to multiple monitors, tubes and wires. They were too fragile to even hold, and I was too exhausted and weak to stay long on my first visit. After a short time, the nurses took me back to my bed.

Both of the boys were on respirators helping them breathe, but within the first day Brennan stabilized and was put on a nasal cannula—a tiny plastic tube delivering oxygen into his nose. I didn't have any idea of the seriousness of Jarrott's condition. The doctors communicated with us, but I was so dazed from medication and dealing with my own recovery those first few days, it didn't sink in with me. Although the boys were tiny, their features were so beautiful and perfect. Little button noses, feet barely an inch long, they looked exactly alike and were so precious.

While I was relieved to be released from the hospital three days after delivery, I knew we wouldn't be bringing the boys home for quite some time, and it was hard leaving them to drive the seventy miles back home. I hated being so far from them. But I was anxious to see McKenzie and knew I'd recover better sleeping at home

Also, Joel's free-spirited youngest sister, Kim, was getting married the next day in Paonia and we were hoping to be at the wedding. I knew I wouldn't feel well, but I was determined to be there. Our extended Millermon family didn't get together as often as we'd like and I knew everyone would be attending. I didn't want to miss the excitement or the family reunion.

Never had it felt so good to sleep in my own bed. But our rest was cut short when the phone rang very early the next morning. It was Dr. Ann Olewnik, one of our neonatologists from the NICU, who'd been present at the boys' birth. My heart sank when I heard her voice on the other line.

"Ginger," she started urgently, "it's Ann Olewnik. I'm sorry to call so early, but I think we're going to have to transfer Jarrott to Denver Children's Hospital."

"What happened?" I whispered, tears already clogging my throat.

"He had a terrible night and he's not doing well. I think he needs to be on an Oscillator ventilator. It will be much gentler on his lungs. We don't have one here." She paused.

"I'm making some calls to Denver and we're watching him closely. I just wanted you to be aware because you need to start thinking about coming down here and either you or Joel flying with him to Denver." She explained that the Oscillator ventilator was a high-frequency ventilator that delivered short, gentle puffs of breath. While Jarrott was already on the conventional ventilator, she hoped the Oscillator would create less damage to his fragile lungs.

I told her we'd begin preparing and hung up the phone in stunned disbelief. I relayed Dr. Olewnik's words to Joel and we lay in tired misery and tears trying to decide what to do if Jarrott had to go. I was still too sore and weak from surgery to travel, so we agreed Joel would take the medical flight with Jarrott. My parents were asleep in our guest room, but before we even got up to tell them the news Joel and I had a time of prayer asking God to stabilize Jarrott so he could stay in Grand Junction. Denver was 250 miles east over the Continental Divide, which runs along the crest at the top of the rugged Rocky Mountains. The drive over the passes was long and, especially in the winter, could be treacherous. We didn't know how we were going to manage having two premature babies in different hospitals clear across the state from each other and neither one close to home.

We woke up my parents and started packing Joel a bag. Within half an hour, Dr. Olewnik called back.

"He's going. The medical flight will be here within an hour and if you're not here, they're going to have to leave without you. He needs to get there as soon as possible. He's not doing well."

Within minutes we were on our way. My brother and sister-in-law, Bob and Jacquie, had arrived from Kansas for the birth of the boys. Jacquie jumped in the car with us for the trip to Grand Junction. I'll never forget hanging on for dear life with a pillow to my stomach to cushion the bumps as Joel raced down the highway. The drive usually took well over an hour, but no way was he was going to miss that flight! Riding in the car sent spirals of pain through my incision and abdomen, but I was afraid if I didn't get to Grand Junction to tell Jarrott goodbye, I would never see him again. The gravity of his situation was finally starting to sink in for us.

When we arrived at the hospital, we hurried to the NICU and washed up. We were brand new to the requirements of the two-minute hand wash when checking into the NICU. It would quickly become a familiar routine.

Dr. Olewnik, tall and thin with short brown hair and clear green eyes, again explained the details of Jarrott's condition and transfer. In the short time we'd been at St. Mary's, I was already impressed with this kind, extremely brilliant woman. Not one for many extra words, Dr. Olewnik spoke to us about the boys' condition and we listened carefully, knowing everything she said was pertinent.

The flight crew arrived shortly after we did, pushing in a portable isolette—a small plastic box on a stretcher that would keep Jarrott secured for the flight. We checked on Brennan, who was resting peacefully, swaddled in a blanket, and then went to Jarrott's side. He was visibly struggling to breathe and his little body trembled. Tears clouded my eyes when the nurse told me I couldn't even touch him.

"He's very over-stimulated right now, Ginger. Even stroking his head or touching his hand sends his heart rate out of control. I'm sorry, you'll just have to look at him."

As the paramedics and nurses prepared for the transfer, I stood next to his warmer as tears coursed down my cheeks.

"I love you, Jarrott," I whispered. "I didn't even get to know you, but I love you so much. Mommy will be praying for you." It was sheer agony to see them roll him away and put him on that flight. Joel and I quickly hugged and said goodbye. We didn't know when we'd see each other again. In my heart, I was convinced I was seeing Jarrott alive for the last time. I was struggling to deal with the fact that I was losing a son I had never even held in my arms.

As Joel and Jarrott began their flight to Denver, my dad and Jacquie drove me back to Paonia. When we left Grand Junction, Kim and Andy's wedding was starting in an hour. So we found ourselves once again racing against the clock to make it in time. I was in no shape physically or mentally at that point to celebrate, but I knew it was really bothering Joel that he was missing his youngest sister's special day. They were close and it was tearing him up to be absent for any reason. I promised him I would be there for both of us.

Traffic was slow heading back and we realized we'd never make it on time. The ceremony was being held in a quiet park beside a stream and the guests had all arrived. We were staying in touch with Joel's family on a cell phone and called when we were about twenty minutes away. They promised to hold off as long as possible. I couldn't believe it when we were moments away and got stopped by a train! I completely gave up on attending. I was so surprised when we screeched up to the park. They had waited! They postponed for almost half an hour until we arrived. The wedding was beautiful and yet it was a bittersweet day as I watched the blessing of a new family beginning even as my heart was breaking for Jarrott.

The next few weeks passed in a blur of misery and exhaustion for us. I made almost daily trips the seventy miles to Grand Junction. Brennan was stabilizing and doing well, but still too tiny and weak to nurse. So I was pumping breast milk and freezing it for both of the boys. The milk was dripped into Brennan's tummy with a nasogastric tube while the nurses worked slowly to teach him to nipple a bottle.

Brennan's doctors encouraged skin-to-skin holding, so I often sat in the rocking chair for hours, cuddling him against my skin. He obviously loved the close contact as I whispered and sang and napped with him. Every day he got a little stronger and a little more alert. Soon he was gaining weight and keeping his body temperature up enough to be moved from under the warmer to an isolette. The next step for him was to be moved to an open crib and learn how to eat before he could come home. Dr. Olewnik was very happy with his steady progress and, as tiny as he was, his little lungs seemed to improve every day.

Joel, on the other hand, was having quite a different experience in Denver. The doctors had immediately put Jarrott on the Oscillator ventilator, which delivered several hundred breaths per minute. The short, gentle puffs of oxygen it pumped into Jarrott's lungs shook his whole body. Joel told me it was terrible to watch him tremble and shake. In those first few days, it seemed nothing could go right for him! His warmer quit overnight and the technical failure wasn't noticed until his body temperature was dangerously low. Another day his IV was mixed incorrectly and he got a drastic overdose of potassium. On top of that, he fought against the ventilator and more than once pulled the tube from his lungs, extubating himself. Each one of these instances set back any progress he was making and was extremely frustrating and discouraging for both Jarrott's medical team and us.

Joel slept in a little cubicle provided for the parents and called me several times a day from the "Bear Phone." Children's Hospital had a comfortable parent lounge and a phone shaped like a bear where families could call long distance for free to quickly update their loved ones on their child's condition. Neither Joel nor I had cell phones at this point, so the use of the "Bear Phone" was a tremendous help to us.

I felt extremely helpless being so far from Jarrott when he was so critical. And it was hard to know Joel was all alone in a city where he didn't know anyone, carrying the burden of staying by Jarrott's bedside nearly twenty-four hours a day.

One of the nurses at St. Mary's had a wonderful suggestion for me one day as I held Brennan. Since I couldn't be with Jarrott, she suggested I tuck a hankie close to my skin for a day so it would carry my scent. Then I went home that afternoon and recorded a tape for Jarrott, softly singing Sunday School songs and reading Bible stories. I told him over and over how much I loved him and that I was praying for him. I mailed a package off to Joel for him to tuck the hankie next to Jarrott and play the tape in his isolette. The effects were amazing! Jarrott's nurses were astounded at how his heart rate would calm and he'd open his eyes wide and look around when Mommy was singing to him. It was an incredible balm to my heart to know that although I wasn't there holding him, I was at least doing something tangible to bring him comfort.

After ten days of being apart, my mom, McKenzie and I drove to Denver. Unbelievably, in the middle of all our drama, my parents' new home in Kansas had flooded and Mom needed to head home to assess the damage and help my dad clean up the mess. She dropped me off at the hospital in Denver and took McKenzie with her to Kansas. My mommy's heart seemed to break every time I had to say goodbye to one of my children! I'd left Brennan in the hospital in the very good hands of his sweet nurses. My sister-in-law, Melissa, also lived in Grand Junction and was happy to spend time in the NICU with him. However, she had her own toddlers, Jamie and Caleb, to attend to so I knew her time with Brennan would be limited. God so graciously provided us with an amazing medical team at St. Mary's and several of Brennan's nurses actually attended the church where Joel's brother, Steve, was a pastor. As hard as it was to leave him, it was so comforting to me to be able to leave Brennan in their hands.

So by the second week of our journey, Brennan was in Grand Junction, Jarrott was in Denver and McKenzie was in Kansas. It was impossible to guess when we'd be back together as a family.

My arms were *aching* to hold Jarrott. I couldn't wait to get into the NICU at Children's and see him. He was off in a little corner in the open nursery underneath a warmer, still unable to regulate his body temperature. Joel warned me how hard it would be to see his miniature body shaking with the Oscillator ventilator and he had not exaggerated the difficulty of seeing Jarrott suffer. I stood beside his bed in tears and again wondered how long he'd survive. He wasn't stable enough when I arrived to hold him so I still had to wait, sitting for twelve hours a day or more beside his bed. Singing, praying, hoping, waiting.

Often I sat in the chair next to him and journaled, trying to make sure I captured every step of this new chapter in our lives. I remember the tightness in my chest and heaviness in my heart as I penned these words:

> Let me now say that this has been the most terrifying, emotional, tired, hectic and traumatic time of my life. A hopelessness encases me occasionally as a parent that my children are not well, close to death even at times, and there is not a solitary thing I can do other than pray. And pray I do. Actually, beg is probably a better word sometimes. A tight, clogged throat, an aching heart, nausea from worrying, a knot in my stomach

these are all very physical things I have felt. As for emotional grief stricken, hopeless, traumatized, weepy, irritable, and exhausted. I think Joel and I have had some of our best and worst days together. Best when we communicate and grieve or rejoice together. Worst when we're exhausted and keep our fears and frustrations bottled up inside but...I know when it's all said and done, we will be much stronger for it.

The day I penned those words, I could never have known what already seemed an intolerable, traumatic situation, would soon go from bad to worse.

I don't know how much longer
I can carry this pain
I need You more than ever
To get me through this thing
I'm past the point of breaking
It's more than I can take
Will You, Would You
Speak peace
Speak peace to me...

Chapter Four

August 1996

WHEN I ARRIVED IN Denver, arrangements for our lodging had been made with St. Christopher House—a beautiful, Victorian-themed hospitality house set up for families who had loved ones in one of the Denver-area hospitals. Similar to an extended-stay hotel, a small kitchen was provided on the ground floor to cook simple meals, and a security guard was available at all hours to walk us the few blocks to the hospital. We weren't situated in one of the best neighborhoods in Denver, so we appreciated that service as we often came back to the room late at night after twelve or fifteen hours at the hospital.

My second day in Denver, Joel and I decided to get out for an hour and go to lunch. We'd not spent time together or even seen each other outside the stress of the hospital for several weeks. One of the nurses had suggested a nice quiet deli on busy Colorado Avenue. Lunch hour traffic was stop-and-go as we tried to find the deli. We finally found the street we thought it was on and both looked away from the road at the same time for the briefest second. When we looked up, we were horrified to see traffic had come to a complete standstill and we had no time to stop. Our little Mazda slammed into the back of a large SUV with a trailer hitch. I cried in pain as the seatbelt pulled hard against my tender incision from the C-section.

We sat there in disbelief! Neither of us had ever been in a car wreck or even received a speeding ticket. The timing of this wreck was almost inconceivable with everything else transpiring in our lives.

Thankfully, the gentleman we hit wasn't angry or irrational and treated us with exceptional kindness. His car wasn't damaged, but his trailer hitch had gone clear into our transmission. We'd nearly totaled our car. As we waited for the police, Joel and I both fought tears and Joel was completely disgusted with himself. I'm pretty sure our exhaustion and state of mind at this point in our lives hadn't helped either one of us be alert enough on the road.

Again, God was gracious and sent us an understanding police officer. He felt terrible about our situation and even showed us pictures of his grandkids. He called a tow truck for us and wasn't going to ticket Joel until we discovered our insurance card had expired the day before. In all the stress of our lives, I hadn't realized they'd expired. The new cards were sitting on the kitchen counter in Paonia. We had a heavy fine to pay and with all of the expenses piling up, it was an added burden that seemed unreal.

The tow truck came to get the car and, not knowing anyone in Denver, we asked him to take us to the hospital and drop us off. Honestly, you can't get much lower than we felt that day! It was really starting to seem like we weren't going to get a break in anything.

But as He always does, God already had a plan to take care

of us. Joel had been given the number of an ex-professional football player named Ross Ritter. Ross was a huddle coach in the Denver area for Fellowship of Christian Athletes and Joel was the coach for FCA in the Paonia area. Not knowing what else to do, Joel gave him a call. We were now stuck in the city with no transportation. Ross and his wife, Cindy, immediately offered the use of their minivan until our car was fixed. Beyond that, they asked if they could minister to us and treat us to a Colorado Rockies game that evening. It was the first time we'd relaxed and laughed in a long, long time and more importantly, the beginning of a lifelong friendship between our families.

What started out as a horrid day ended beautifully for me that night after the Rockies game. When we got back to the hospital to check on Jarrott, the nurses told me I could finally hold him. It was the first time I got to hold my sweet baby in my arms. It was only for a few, brief moments, but I'll never find words to describe the emotions I felt when I cradled his miniature body next to mine and looked into his face. Such love consumed me and I knew I would do anything in my power to protect him, fight for him and help him survive. I had no idea the length or the fierceness of the battle that lay ahead of us!

While we were watching over Jarrott in Denver, Brennan continued to improve in Grand Junction. His nurses were taking Polaroid pictures of him daily and even mailed pictures of Brennan's first bath. I was relieved he was improving so rapidly, but it was difficult to know I was missing important moments and "firsts" in his little life. It truly was a blessing he was progressing because I'm not sure what I would have done if both the boys had been critically ill. I felt so torn, needing to be with both my babies and McKenzie.

Jarrott slowly started to show some slight improvement.

In fact, we were told if he could get off the Oscillator ventilator, he could be transferred back to St. Mary's and our family would be closer together. We were elated. So we began to fervently pray for Jarrott to stabilize and get off the respirator.

We were crushed when our insurance company informed us they would not cover Jarrott's flight back to Grand Junction. We explained to them how far from home we were, that Brennan was in the other hospital, but it didn't matter. We began to realize Jarrott would be in the hospital indefinitely, 250 miles from home. We had no idea how we were going to survive.

One glimmer of hope arrived on our horizon. We discovered another baby in the NICU in Denver was going to be transferred to Grand Junction within several days. Her insurance was covering the flight, and her parents agreed to let Jarrott share the airplane—they called it a "piggyback flight"—if he was ready to go when she left. Oh, how we prayed! The day before the flight was scheduled, they extubated Jarrott, taking him off the ventilator. We held our breath, hoping he'd remain stable. The doctors still weren't quite convinced he was going to make it off of the respirator and asked the little girl's family to wait one more day before her transfer. They agreed.

On August 27th, exactly three weeks after his birth, Jarrott was flown back to St. Mary's Hospital while Joel and I drove over the mountain passes to meet him. I was so anxious to see Brennan again!

That very night, I held Brennan and Jarrott in my arms together for the first time. It was incredible. Even as tiny as they were, they were an armful! What a feeling…holding both of my beautiful sons. As excited as I was to hold them both, my heart was heavy looking at the evident differences in the boys. Brennan was gaining weight nicely and his skin was a pink, healthy tone. Jarrott was already smaller, since he had not been thriving and his skin, even on oxygen, was a dusky light purple.

Even with the boys in the same hospital, we had no normalcy in our lives. Although closer than Denver, St. Mary's was still seventy miles from our home. We tried to set some sort of schedule. Many times I'd stay in Grand Junction for two or three days at a time with Steve and Melissa, and Joel would try to stay connected in the ministry and his job at the church in Paonia. At least Grand Junction was close enough for him to make frequent trips and still fulfill his duties at the church. But there was simply no routine for us. McKenzie floated between her two Grandmas' houses and Aunt Melissa's and although she wasn't even two, she had an extensive vocabulary and a gypsy heart. She loved to go, go, go all the time, so it really didn't bother her to be spending her days between homes. It was all one big adventure to her, and I think it was a gracious gift of God that she wasn't crying and yearning for me! It would have added to my guilt and distress at being pulled in more directions than I could possibly go.

I never knew what a tremendous blessing it would be that we lived right across the street from Joel's parents. Even before the boys were born, we spent a lot of time at their house, eating meals and enjoying his folks and his sister, Kathy, who lived right down the street. While most of my friends shuddered at the prospect of living across the street from their in-laws, I loved it. I found a wonderful companion in my fun mother-in-law, Carol, and one of the highlights of my day would be to make some outrageous comment and see her throw back her head in laughter. And since Mom Millermon had reared six kids, she always had great advice on parenting for me. I most definitely learned that just about anything that ails you should be soaked in Epsom salt.

Joel had the great privilege of working in ministry with his dad, who had been the pastor at Bible Center Church for over thirty years. Gray-haired, wise and soft-spoken, it took me a while to figure out how ornery Dad Millermon really was. Once I got over being intimidated by his quiet demeanor, however, Dad and I were constantly trying to one-up each other with prank phone calls and practical jokes. It was a balm to my heart knowing McKenzie was used to being at Grandma Millermon's house a lot, so it didn't seem out of the ordinary for her to spend extra time there while I was at the hospital with the boys.

Brennan continued to improve and at seven weeks old, he was released to go home. It was a wonderful day, putting him in his little car seat to go home. He was barely over four pounds and so tiny. He was still quite fragile and we knew we'd have to guard him from viruses and illness. He came home on a nasal cannula of oxygen and a heart/apnea monitor. The monitors kept track of any dangerous changes in his heart rate or breathing difficulty. Brennan still had spells of forgetting to breathe (a condition called apnea) and we needed to watch that closely. He also needed breathing treatments three times a day and many small feedings because he could only tolerate a few ounces at a time. My mom came back from Kansas to help and Joel's parents were available as well. It took a lot of teamwork to figure out how to care for a fussy preemie at home!

One of the funniest memories I have of Brennan's homecoming was that all the ladies in the church were dying to see him. No one had been allowed in the NICU, so they all wanted to dote on this little boy they'd been praying for. Well, we had to be extremely careful of germs and viruses, so no way could we let them hold him or expose him to illness. I laughed hysterically when Joel suggested we wrap Saran wrap over his bassinet so they could look at him, but not breathe on him. We quickly nixed that idea, as air supply was an issue! But then Joel came up with a great solution. We had a big picture window in our dining room at the parsonage. We bundled Brennan up and laid him on the cushioned window seat while all the ladies in the church came by in a single file line to look at him through the window. These faithful women had prayed and prayed for our boys, so it was a special thing for them to get a look at him, even if they couldn't hold him.

By October we were still in a daily struggle with Jarrott. Dr. Olewnik had told us early in our hospital stay that life with a preemie as sick as Jarrott would be a rollercoaster, and she wasn't kidding! One day we'd be elated to find out he'd gained an ounce. The next day we'd find out the weight had actually been fluid on his lungs and he needed to get rid of it. We began to realize that unless he started to gain some healthy weight, he'd be right back on the ventilator. Every day we'd go into the NICU with our hopes high that he'd had a restful, good night and was still breathing on his own. Many mornings our hopes were dashed as we came in to find him intubated and on the ventilator again.

Joel and I were giving blood as often as we could to store up for Jarrott since he needed multiple transfusions. His body couldn't keep his blood count up and by the time he was three months old he'd had at least six transfusions. His eyes were also a concern and were checked weekly. This was another complication for a preemie and the longer he was on high amounts of oxygen, the more damage was being done to his eyes. He was very close to needing surgery, which could only be done in Denver. I was nervous every time the ophthalmologist came by to check him.

The last week in October, things started to unravel. Jarrott had a great week previously and seemed to be improving. We had so much hope. He was extubated—off the respirator—for a week and was doing beautifully. He was moved to an open crib for the first time, a big step for getting ready for home. However, around midnight on October 26, my 25th birthday, he fell apart. His need for oxygen shot up dramatically. By four o'clock Sunday morning he was back on the ventilator and his lung x-rays indicated pneumonia. He was put back in an isolette, having only tolerated the open crib a few days, and we were back at square one. The doctors started him on antibiotics and steroids, and we waited. No words could express our disappointment at his relapse.

That setback dimmed in comparison when a week later I found myself in the cockpit of a tiny plane, making the medical flight over the mountains in the dark, with nurses assisting Jarrott in the back. It was a bumpy, cold flight. I knew the mountains below us were already covered with snow. His doctors in Grand Junction had determined Jarrott needed a bronchoscopy and that could only be done by a pediatric pulmonologist in Denver. They needed to put a scope into his airways and lungs to determine exactly what was going on, to more fully diagnose what we were up against.

I felt like I couldn't take it. We were going back to Denver. The very thing I had been dreading and begging God not to allow to happen. I was starting to lose hope in my journey and struggled to remember God was sovereign. Heading back to Denver alone, away from my family was not helping my outlook, and I felt myself sliding into depression. I had always been an upbeat, optimistic person so this battle with hopelessness was new to me. The road God was calling our family to walk was rugged and as we'd see very soon, we were heading into some of the darkest days of our lives.

Mercy Seat
By Jeremy Johnson, Paul Marino and Ginger Millermon
Adapted from the hymn, "From Every Stormy Wind That Blows"
by Hugh Stowell

From every stormy wind that blows
From every swelling tide of woes
There is a calm, a sure retreat
Found beneath the mercy seat...

"May the God of hope fill you with all joy and peace
as you trust in Him,
so that you may overflow with hope
by the power of the Holy Spirit."

—Romans 15:13

Part II

Chapter Five

_____

October 1996

I FLEW TO DENVER with Jarrott late Sunday night. We got him settled into an isolette, and I was finally able to crash on a cot in the women's sleep room. When I woke up Monday morning, I was feeling sick. I'm sure my immune system was so worn down by this point, I couldn't fight off the countless viruses floating around the hospital. By Monday night I had a terrible sore throat and was absolutely miserable. There is nothing worse than being sick and far from home.

I had a horrible day. I went into the nursery early, wearing a mask and washing often. Jarrott's nurse on duty that day had floated from another area and wasn't as familiar with his needs as I would've liked. I spent the day paging her to turn his oxygen up because his oxygen saturation levels were not where I knew his doctors in Grand Junction had wanted them to be. It was an incredibly frustrating time as the nursery was understaffed, and I didn't feel like he was getting enough attention and care. I'm sure I was driving the nurses and staff crazy, but I felt like I had to constantly monitor Jarrott and stay on top of things to keep him safe. I was sick and exhausted, but no way was I leaving his side. I called my parents and my dad started the eight-hour drive to the hospital to help me. When he arrived Tuesday morning, I was so thankful to see him and have his help keeping a close eye on Jarrott's care.

Jarrott's bronchoscopy and x-rays went well on Tuesday. That morning's x-ray showed his lungs were very wet and retaining fluid so he was given the medication Lasix to help his body flush out the extra fluid. His bronchoscopy held surprising results for us—his airways and lungs didn't look quite as bad as the doctors had anticipated. The main problem they could see was his upper airways were floppy and narrow so air was not moving well. They also did a barium swallow to see if the liquid he was swallowing when he took a bottle was going into his lungs. The doctors were dismayed, but not surprised, to see he was regurgitating and aspirating his stomach contents right into his lungs. This serious reflux and aspiration problem certainly explained the bouts of pneumonia and lung difficulties. The solution to his reflux, however, was not a simple one. With the condition being severe, medication was not going to cure it. Jarrott needed major stomach surgery. With this news, Joel was quickly on his way to be with us in Denver.

As we waited for Jarrott's surgery over the next several days, we were having a whole different set of problems with Brennan. We were back at the St. Christopher House in a nice, clean room so that was a huge improvement over sleeping on a cot in the hospital. But Brennan was having difficulty eating and was throwing up almost every feeding. He was fussy and discontented, and sometimes cried nearly twenty hours a day. People would see us in the elevator at St. Christopher House with Brennan and recognize his scream.

Their eyes would narrow and they'd say, "Oh! This is the baby who's been crying all night!" He was keeping the whole place up! His heart/apnea monitors also went off frequently at night so we were getting very little sleep.

We had no idea what to do with him. He was off his oxygen for a short time, and it was so much easier toting him around without the oxygen tank. But within a day or two he was in the emergency room at Children's, struggling to breathe with a heart rate way too high. So he was right back on the oxygen and needing more breathing treatments throughout the day. I could barely keep up with all the treatments and feedings before this bout, and things kept getting more complicated. Preemies are typically fussy and need a quiet, predictable routine…and we had neither. We weren't comfortable leaving him with anyone since he was still on the monitors and oxygen, so we took him to the NICU with us every day. It was a noisy, overstimulating place for both him and Jarrott.

After a few weeks being back in Denver, McKenzie came to spend several days with us. Though it was so wonderful to see her and spend time with her, she was too young and active to stay in our tiny hotel room for very long. After about three days she was climbing the walls and bored to tears. Fortunately, a wonderful lady named Mildred ran the front desk at St. Christopher House. She was sassy and funny, and McKenzie loved visiting with her. We'd take her down the elevator just to see Mildred and all the way down McKenzie would call out, "Midrid! Here I come, Midrid!" As hard as it was to keep McKenzie busy and happy, she brought much needed laughter into our lives when she was with us. She was our ray of sunshine during a dark, dark time.

One afternoon as we ate lunch at a fast food restaurant, McKenzie hopped out of our booth and shot across the room before we could catch her. Next thing we knew, she was several booths down, perched across from an elderly man sitting all alone. I think she thought he looked lonely. I was going to grab her and apologize when I noticed the look on the man's face. He was completely charmed and thrilled with the curly-haired little girl sitting across from him. McKenzie grinned at him for a minute and then proceeded to talk his ears off and ask him a dozen questions. He loved it and she made his day. I still think it's amazing how many times I've observed my children having a sensitive heart to others when I'm too busy to notice and overlook a need.

It was so sweet and refreshing to have McKenzie with us, but she couldn't be in the NICU, so that made it very hard to spend the time we needed watching over Jarrott. After several days of McKenzie visiting, Jacquie came to get her and take her back to Kansas for a short time.

November 5th was our nation's election day and Jarrott's surgery date. Needless to say, this was one election we didn't get to vote! We did spend time in prayer that day for our nation and the decisions that would be affecting our country with the election of our new president. We were up early at the hospital to see Jarrott before they took him in to surgery. His procedure was called a Nissen fundoplication. The doctors were wrapping the top of his stomach to create a smaller opening between the stomach and esophagus. While there, they took the opportunity to insert a gastric tube and perform a procedure on his digestive tract to make it drain faster. While he was under, Jarrott was also being scoped again and having laser surgery on some mucosa in his nasal passages. Multiple complications could occur, and the doctors had spent ample time explaining these before surgery. They also explained that because Jarrott was so small, it would be difficult to get things perfect. I couldn't image all of the intricate surgeries and work being done on such a tiny little body. It was the day before his three-month birthday, and he was a little over six pounds.

The surgeries took hours, and Joel and I passed the time sitting in the parent lounge praying, reading and calling our loved ones on the "Bear Phone" to keep them updated. Just when I thought I couldn't stand waiting much longer, Jarrott was out of surgery and doing well. It was very sobering to be led back to the NICU and see him still sedated on the ventilator. He had gauze and bandages covering his incisions, but we could see the scar ran from his chest to his belly button. I was glad they were keeping him asleep...hoping some of the pain would pass before he had to wake up.

The next several weeks continued to be a rollercoaster for us. And at some point, the hospital social worker sat us down for a serious talk.

"I wanted to visit with you about a few things today," she started. "You know half of all marriages in America end in divorce." We nodded, a little puzzled by the direction of the conversation. She continued.

"Well, when you have twins, that statistic goes up another twenty percent. And when you have a special needs child like Jarrott, it soars another twenty-five percent." She paused. "That leaves a five-percent chance of your marriage surviving."

Now, I have to admit—her little speech was starting to tick me off. I waited with a raised eyebrow for her to get to the point.

"I'm telling you this because you have to take care of your marriage. You have some very tough times ahead of you, and if you don't take care of your relationship, who is going to take care of Jarrott? Who will be here for him? We see families fall apart in here all the time. Don't let it happen to you," she urged us.

She left Joel and me alone after a few more minutes and we sat and looked at each other. I could see her point. The stress was unbelievable. But we determined right then and there we were not, absolutely *not*, going to be a statistic. We would not be another failed marriage. We verbally agreed we'd work things out and never use the "D" word in our marriage. Divorce would never even be spoken of as an option, no matter how difficult things got. We agreed not to take out our stress on each other, and we'd invest time and love into our relationship instead of letting the trials tear us apart. We knew it would be tough, but not impossible with the strength we had in our relationship with the Lord. I will honestly tell you these words were much easier said than done through the days that were to come.

The days immediately following Jarrott's surgery seemed to be much smoother. I'd sit for hours and have "skin-to-skin" contact with him sleeping right against me. He seemed to rest and be so comfortable as I held him. One of the moms in the nursery who also had a tiny preemie shared a Scripture with me one day that had been such an encouragement to her. I wrote these verses in my journal,

> "You turned my wailing into dancing; you removed my sackcloth and clothed me with joy, that my heart may sing to you and not be silent. O Lord my God, I will give you thanks forever." Psalm 30:11-12.

There were definitely days I struggled to find anything to be thankful for. But then I had to recall and remember as tough as things were, we still had Jarrott and he was still fighting hard to survive. Some days were better than others, but over the next week after his surgery, we seemed to be on a path to recovery and healing. The doctors were hopeful that since he'd no longer be eating by mouth, but through his stomach tube, he wouldn't have any more issues with aspirating into his lungs. They felt his lungs would now start to improve and heal. We were encouraged to learn through this process that children will grow new lung tissue until they are seven to ten years old. That meant while Jarrott's lungs were not good at this point, with better nutrition and keeping the damage of pneumonia away, he had a good chance to have healthy lungs. We clung to that hope!

Our smooth sailing lasted about one week before we started to see some things that really concerned us. As with all hospitals, the setting and the staffing were not always ideal. For the most part, Jarrott was receiving impeccable, loving care, but he had no consistency in his nursing staff. Someone new was caring for him almost every day, not always knowing the best way to deal with him. With a NICU as large as Children's, many babies needed to be cared for with not always quite enough staff. I was a very non-confrontational person at this point in my life and hated having to speak up if I felt like things weren't right. But Jarrott inspired in me a fierce protective side, and I began to work my way up the chain of command, insisting firmly but politely that things had to improve in his care. I was trembling in my boots the day I had a meeting with the head nursing staff and several nurses who had been caring for Jarrott. I stated my concerns in that meeting and was accused by one nurse of being too demanding. I apologized and realized maybe I was demanding, but it was my responsibility to make sure Jarrott was taken care of in the best manner possible.

That difficult meeting ended up being one of the most positive things that happened to us during this time. Jarrott was finally put into a private room instead of being in the open nursery with all of the monitors and babies screaming twenty-four hours a day. All of the noise and commotion constantly overstimulated him and made it very difficult for him to rest. He was also given a care team consisting of nurses we mostly handpicked and felt comfortable with. The difference we saw almost immediately was phenomenal. The attention he received was a drastic improvement and we were relieved at the consistency of communicating to the same team of nurses.

This was a real growing-up time for me, having to stick to my guns and get things done I knew were appropriate for Jarrott's benefit. I hated it, sometimes cried and whined about it, but God gave me the inner strength to confront what needed to be confronted and fight for Jarrott's care. I believe some of the difficulties I went through as a teenager were a precursor to prepare me for these bigger, life-changing trials. I had battled through some tough peer situations as a teen and had even tried to take my life as a fifteen-year-old girl. However, God protected me through that time and helped me realize He would be faithful and He was enough for me. Nothing else really mattered. The maturity that began in my spiritual walk as a lonely teenager kept me from crumbling as an adult facing an enormous crisis.

As God continued to refine and mature me, hopelessness and depression took a back burner in my life, and I began to fully realize how much Jarrott needed me to protect him. I have found when I quit focusing so much on how *I* feel and the things that bother *me*, and instead turn my attention to the needs of others, my circumstances begin to not look so bad. Many times it's not my situation that needs to change, it's my heart.

…Even in the shadow of the valley
Your light will reach into the darkest place
Even when a heart is cold and empty
And it feels like hope is ending
Your love remains
You are beautiful…

Chapter Six

_____

November 1996

November 17

I want to beg the Lord to PLEASE let us just go home! We are so tired of living in a hotel, eating fast food or microwave food. We just want to be home and together. It would be so nice to spend Thanksgiving at home as a family.

On Wednesday Jarrott was getting his tube retaped and managed to extubate himself. He was under a hood for twenty-four hours then was put on a nasal cannula. He's still on the cannula. He's actually had a very good week! He and Brennan have been able to spend some time together in Jarrott's bed. Jarrott LOVES to snuggle up with Brennan. Brennan is doing so well. He's a real cutie with his bright blue eyes. The boys are so adorable together. I could never love two little boys more. I look so forward to the day, maybe a year from now, when the boys are all caught up and normal, active babies. I long and pray for that day!

November 18

We were dealt quite a crushing blow today. The doctor called at 5:45 AM to tell us that Jarrott was re-intubated. We were SO disappointed! Actually, we still are. His carbon dioxide was 85 and he was really working hard to breathe. If he continued to work that hard, his heart would eventually quit. His x-rays show that the upper right lobe of his lung has collapsed.

This was our life. These were typical journal entries for me. One day we'd be excited and hopeful with weight gain, oxygen saturation, blood work, and ventilator settings. The next day everything would crash and the doctors would be working just to keep him breathing.

As we struggled to understand why he'd deprogressed so dramatically, we were horrified to find out an occupational therapist had misread the doctor's orders and had tried to feed him a bottle. Just twenty-four hours later he was back on the ventilator with a partially collapsed lung. We suspected pneumonia from aspiration, but our concerns were downplayed and our nurse actually suggested we go home for a few days to de-stress. No way were we leaving him! These were times when we found it the most difficult to cope with Jarrott's sickness—when mistakes were made and Jarrott suffered for it. We watched as other families in the neonatal nursery got angry with the medical staff and threatened to sue over various issues. Sometimes it was incredibly hard to keep our attitudes in check and forgive when we knew things weren't done as well as they should have been. I struggled to know when to speak up for Jarrott's safety and when to let things go.

We wanted so much to keep a good testimony and not get a reputation for being difficult, but at times we had to put Jarrott's welfare above what people thought of us. We made it a goal to do everything politely and calmly and as non-confrontational as possible. It wasn't always easy. I vented a lot in my journal and on many entries I can tell how angry and fed-up I was by my handwriting. One particularly hard day I wrote,

> They think we're stressing out and overreacting when all we are doing is asking legitimate questions and expecting honest answers! We deserve to know what's going on with our child and that is not a right that I will give up for ANYONE!

A few days after that frustrated entry, Jarrott was stabilizing and was again taken off the ventilator. We had another care conference with the doctors, nurses and caseworker to be sure we were all on the same page concerning Jarrott's care. After that meeting and with Jarrott stabilized, we finally felt comfortable enough to go home for a day or two. It had been several weeks since I had been able to be in my house, get fresh clothes and even get caught up on mail and bills. It was an incredible feeling to be home, sleeping in my own bed! That first night we were home, for the first time in my life, I walked in my sleep and almost fell down a flight of stairs. It was a small indicator to me of the tremendous stress I was enduring.

McKenzie was beside herself with joy that we were all

home together. It had been many weeks since we'd had any type of a normal family time. We laughed and played and spent time at the park shuffling through autumn leaves. It was a time our family desperately needed.

Also very needed for me was the opportunity to attend church that Sunday. It had been at least six weeks or more since I had been able to go to church. It was a balm to my soul to receive all of the hugs and kisses of the wonderful people in our church family. I knew many of them were faithfully lifting us up in prayer. I had no doubt their prayers were helping to sustain us. They'd been so supportive and kind as Joel made weekly trips to Denver to spend time with the boys and me. Most weeks he'd drive to Denver on Monday and spend a few days, then return later in the week to work at the church and try to stay connected with the teenagers. He was so torn, wanting to be at the hospital all the time, but also needing to work. It was frustrating and discouraging to both of us, but we knew our ordeal was going to be long and drawn out and neither one of us wanted the ministry in Paonia to suffer.

The drive back to Denver that weekend was beautiful. Winding through Glenwood Canyon and up and over the summit of Vail Pass was always breathtaking, no matter the time of year. It was evident in the high country that winter was coming and I knew it was going to get more and more difficult for Joel to make the drive over the Rocky Mountains every week once the snow started.

I was anxious to reach the hospital and see how Jarrott was doing. We'd been calling in often to check on him and he'd remained stable while we were gone. So we were shocked to walk into the NICU and see nurses surrounding his bed. My heart sank as I recognized almost instantly he was struggling for every breath. He was still off the ventilator, but it was obvious he was not breathing well on his own. Joel and I asked questions and stood by his bed as we watched him struggle. He was severely retracting with every breath, his little tummy caving in around his ribs. I was not expecting the conversation we had in the next few moments with his doctors.

The neonatologist on call that evening spoke up. "We've been waiting for you to get here. You need to make the decision whether or not to put Jarrott back on the ventilator."

I looked up in surprise. This had never been our decision before. Jarrott's medical team had always decided and reintubated him when they thought he needed it, whether we were present or not.

"It's our decision? Why is this our decision this time?" I was confused!

The doctor hesitated, "This was Jarrott's last chance to thrive off the vent. If we reintubate him, he's going to need a tracheotomy. You need to decide if this is what you want for Jarrott and for you."

Joel and I looked at each other, our hearts sinking. We'd been hoping to avoid a tracheotomy. We understood through previous conversations that if Jarrott underwent the surgery for a trach, he'd likely have it for several years. This seemed incredibly daunting to me. Joel and I had spent a little bit of time with a family in our community who had premature triplets. One of their little girls was trached and we visited their home to see what that was like. All the equipment and tubing seemed so complicated to me. I thought I could never figure out how to have a child at home who was so medically dependent. I kept thinking it would not happen to us! But here we were at a crossroads and burdened with this enormous decision.

We stood by his bed that Sunday evening in November and pleaded with the Lord for wisdom. This was not a decision that was easy or that we knew how to make on our own. We prayed and agonized beside his bed for over four hours, watching his tiny chest cave in as he struggled to breath. His heart rate did not go under 180 beats per minute during those long hours. His body was working so hard. Too hard.

Finally, sometime after midnight, we made the toughest decision we'd had to make for Jarrott. We had them put him back on the ventilator. We requested for him to be reintubated with the full knowledge he'd soon be undergoing surgery for a tracheotomy.

Two days later on November 26, 1996, two days before Thanksgiving, Jarrott went in for his tracheotomy. We found ourselves again in the surgery waiting room for hours, hoping the doctors would come out and tell us he came through the surgery.

I wrote in my journal as I waited.

It was one of the hardest decisions we've ever made. He may have the trach for up to two years! It was so hard to commit him to this but he really wasn't going to breathe on his own without a ventilator. With the vent in his throat instead of his mouth, he can suck on his pacifier (his favorite pastime!) smile, move his head and pretty much act like a normal baby. It will be very inconvenient for us, hauling all of his stuff around, but we have peace knowing it is best for him and he is in our Father's hands.

This has been SUCH an emotional time for us! It's getting harder and harder to leave McKenzie time after time. We want so badly to be at home as a family. Maybe soon.

Even reading back on that journal entry, I shake my head. I was so naïve and had no idea how difficult and complicated life would be with a trached baby. There would be nothing normal about it.

Surgery went well on Tuesday, and we were looking forward to my parents coming on Thursday afternoon to spend Thanksgiving with us. But by Wednesday Jarrott was already struggling again. I couldn't believe it. Even on the ventilator and trach, he was working too hard to breathe and his carbon dioxide level was rising again. By the day after Thanksgiving, he was still not doing well and his blood work showed he had a bacterial infection. His doctors decided to put in an arterial line—a thin tube inserted into an artery— and I stood by his bedside for nearly two hours as his doctor made an incision into his tiny wrist and dug around for the artery. His little body was already covered with scars from the multiple surgeries, many IVs, and previous attempts to find arteries. It was hard watching him go through so much. I had never been one to tolerate too much blood, so I was surprised I could stand by and watch as they looked once again for an artery.

By the weekend, although he was on antibiotics, he still wasn't doing well and was covered in a rash. The doctors started to suspect he might have the deadly Respiratory Syncytial Virus. RSV infects the air passages and lungs, and it was a terrifying threat we lived under during the winter months. RSV could cause a simple cold in a healthy person. But this virus could lead to a severe illness that is often fatal in a preemie.

December 5, 1996

We almost lost him yesterday! It was such a shock. I called around 5:00 AM while I was feeding Brennan and they said his heart rate had dropped and they changed his trach. But I guess I didn't realize how serious it was until the nurse practitioner called back and said they were really worried about him. Evidently, in the night, his heart rate dropped suddenly and they tried everything to get it back up. They had to do chest compressions and bag him. It was a very scary day for us.

We did find out that week that Jarrott did not have RSV, so we were relieved. But we also discovered his insurance would not cover the immune globulin Respigam, which would help him not contract the virus in the future. That was to be one of the many things we'd fight the insurance company about over the months. It took an amazing amount of persistence and perseverance to get Jarrott the care and medications he needed.

Later that same week, the doctors discovered Jarrott's bowel was not functioning properly. We kept an eye on his weight every day, hoping for even an ounce of healthy weight gain. We were really disheartened when green fluid started coming out of his gastrostomy tube and his bowels obviously weren't functioning right. The doctors weren't sure at this point if he had a stomach virus or if it was something far more serious. They started to talk to us about the possibility of his bowel shutting down. This would obviously have a devastating effect on his already frail body. It seemed like we'd conquer one battle and another would crop up almost immediately.

In the midst of the trauma we were facing almost daily with Jarrott, we'd made friends with another young couple in the neonatal nursery. Jon and Janelle's firstborn son, Daniel, was born at 1 pound 6 ounces. He was the tiniest thing I had ever seen. We'd sometimes have lunch or dinner with Jon and Janelle and compare days and stories. They were living in the St. Christopher House as well, so we saw them often as we'd come and go from the hospital.

Daniel was a micro-preemie and very critical. It soon became evident this little boy was not going to survive. Joel and I watched with such respect and agony as this wonderful couple came to terms with the imminent death of their firstborn. The day finally came when it was clear Daniel was going home to the Lord. Jon and Janelle called and asked if I would sit with them while he passed away. I will not forget that day and experience as long as I live. It is almost too sacred and too heart-wrenching to put on paper. I stayed with them until the wee hours of the morning as that amazing little boy struggled and his heart rallied then stopped, only to start again. After many agonizing hours, he finally went home.

I went back to my room and curled up under my covers and wept my heart out. Joel was in Paonia that weekend and I was alone, dealing with not only the grief of our friends losing Daniel. But also dealing with the reality it might soon be Joel and me watching Jarrott die. Some thought it was too much, that I shouldn't have put myself through watching Daniel die. But I believe God used my presence in Jon and Janelle's lives and he certainly used their faithfulness and strong faith in mine.

Joel and I dealt with our stress in different ways through all this. I journaled a lot. It was therapeutic to me to put all my burdens, frustrations and victories on paper. There were often things too painful to say out loud that I could say on paper. I also talked through many of my worries and concerns with Joel. I had those thousands of words a day that had to get out somehow!

But it was much harder for Joel to express all he was going through, and many times I wasn't sure how he was doing or if he was coping. Sometimes we'd find ourselves bickering over silly, stupid things only later to realize we were taking out our grief and frustration on each other.

The day after we made the decision to put Jarrott back on the ventilator, the stress and tension between Joel and me was soaring. We returned to the St. Christopher House exhausted and cranky. My mom had left some homemade brownies for us in our hotel room, and Joel was helping himself to one. I'd just vacuumed our room that day. It seems like such a frivolous thing, but since we were long-term tenants at the hospitality house, they didn't clean our room and it was my responsibility to go find a vacuum and clean it. Such a small thing, but on top of everything else it was a pain and I rarely found time to make it a priority. So that morning I'd hunted down the little eighty-year-old Spanish-speaking nun, and through hand motions indicated I needed the vacuum. I hauled it to the third floor and meticulously vacuumed every inch of carpet. It felt so good to do something normal and I loved having a nice clean room.

So as Joel reached for his brownie that evening, he somehow flipped the knife across the room, flinging brownie all over my clean carpet. I was so mad!

"Joel!" I yelled at him, my eyes blazing. "I just vacuumed!" I wanted to throw something at him! I was so frustrated and so tired.

Instead of responding in any way to my anger, Joel froze and looked at that butter knife, stuck to the carpet with brownie frosting. Then he started to smile. His jaw twitched, his big brown eyes sliding over to me. I hadn't seen that ornery look for a long time. And then he snickered. That was it for me. I couldn't help it. I started giggling and pretty soon we were both rolling on the bed in a hysterical fit of laughter.

It really wasn't that funny. But we both recognized we

were completely overstressed and exhausted. And laughter *is* really good medicine.

Shortly after that stress-relieving episode, I went to a bookstore and bought a huge Calvin and Hobbs comic book. I decided we'd better find something to smile about, so we'd sit together at the hospital, often both of us squeezing into the oversized green recliner by Jarrott's bed, and laugh at the childish antics of a little boy and his stuffed cat.

It wasn't profound, wasn't really mature or spiritual or maybe the most amazing use of our time. But we discovered it was a lot more fun—and much healthier—to laugh together to relieve our stress than to argue and bicker and build up the walls between us. From the early days of our courtship and marriage, laughter and teasing and fun had been an integral part of who we were as a couple. We'd lost that in this journey. I was determined that in spite of our circumstances, we had to find a way to have fun together again. Nearly every day, our emotions were on a rollercoaster and it was either laugh or cry. I definitely did plenty of both, but I decided after those first few months it really felt a lot better to laugh than cry, and it was sure a lot less messy!

Love Song
By Ginger Millermon
©Anothen Music 2002

…You're my best friend
On a rainy day
when my tears are close at hand
you're my true love on a sunkissed beach
walking barefoot through the sand
you're my love song
You're my friend…

Chapter Seven

————

December 1996

> *December 24, 1996 Christmas Eve*
> *What a different celebration of Christ's birth we are having this year! Tonight we'll open gifts with my parents, Kenzie and Brennan in our hotel room. We'll be taking Jarrott his gifts too, of course. It's not the same as being at home but we have a little tree and a corner full of gifts. Our stockings are taped to the wall and fall off frequently. We laugh and tape them back up. But you know the BEST thing about this Christmas? We are all together! Our first Christmas with our baby boys.*

I struggled a lot that Christmas to keep a good attitude and not be depressed. I tried to find *something* to be happy about and thankful for. I really just wanted to be at my Grandma's house in Kansas. Grandma and Grandpa Martin's old white farmhouse with green trim was right in the middle of a wheat field that was usually covered with snow around Christmas-time. All the cousins and aunts and uncles would pack into that house and open gifts and drink coffee and eat ridiculous amounts of Aunt Lyndel's meatballs and my mom's fudge brownies. We'd spend the entire day together playing cha-rades and catching up on each other's lives. If it happened to be a warmer than usual Christmas, a competitive game of football would start up in the front yard.

When I looked out our hotel window in downtown Denver, all I could see were brick buildings and gray, dirty snow. It didn't feel like a happy, festive time of year at all to me.

One particular afternoon I was in our little room, looking out the window with tears rolling down my cheeks. I was thinking about all the things we were missing that Christmas that I so looked forward to every year. The programs, the caroling, shopping for gifts, wrapping the kids' toys. We were missing it all. Our finances were unbelievably tight and we were barely keeping our heads above water. In fact, if it weren't for occasional help from friends and loved ones, we wouldn't have been making it financially. Even with a reduced nightly rate on the hospitality house, months on end paying for a hotel room was adding up—as was the gas for Joel traveling back and forth from the hospital to home, 500 miles a trip. We were doing good just being able to buy the tiniest gifts for each other and the kids.

As my tears blinded me, staring out that window, I started to sink into depression again and really feel sorry for myself. Unbidden, that very first Christmas came to mind.

That first Christmas wasn't an ideal situation either! In fact, far from it. First of all, Mary and Joseph were engaged to be married. Actually, they were betrothed, which is heavier than we think of an engagement. It was a covenant made between Mary's and Joseph's families, promising they would be married. Mary was a teenage girl, probably no more than sixteen years old. I often think there must have been such excitement in her home, planning a beautiful wedding. I picture Mary and her mother giggling and planning the dress, the food, and dancing that would accompany a traditional Jewish wedding.

And then it says in Matthew 1:18, "...she was found to be with child..." She was pregnant. An angel had appeared to her and told her she would be pregnant by the Holy Spirit with the Messiah. I can't imagine Mary's conversation with her mother!

"Mom, an angel told me I'm pregnant." That must have gone over well. At least Joseph was also visited by an angel. And instead of accusing Mary, he believed the angel and married her right away, keeping both of their honor intact. Nazareth was not a large town. Word must have swept through the village and had Joseph not acted honorably and swiftly, there would've been devastating consequences in both of their lives, especially Mary's.

A difficult situation gets even worse as Mary nears the time of delivery. There was a sudden requirement to go to Bethlehem to register, and she and Joseph had to make the arduous journey. Here was Mary, nine months pregnant, traveling for hours on a donkey, getting ready to go into labor! She had to be exhausted when they finally arrived in Bethlehem and then there was no place for them to stay. No place to have a baby! That poor, tired young girl had to lie down in a dirty old barn and have her baby. And not just any baby! She bore the King of Kings and the Lord of Lords. And the only ones there to honor this royal birth were Joseph, maybe some barn animals, and a few lowly shepherds.

When I started thinking on all this and how inconvenient, cold and miserable that whole situation had to be for Mary, I started to realize I didn't have it so bad after all. My parents had come to celebrate with us—our little family was together for our first Christmas. It wasn't so bad. Deep in my heart I wondered if it would be the only Christmas we'd have with Jarrott. So I cherished every moment with him.

December 24

Doctors are talking more and more about the fact that there may come a time when there's nothing left to do for him. Joel and I have discussed it as well. It's so easy to say the words, "he may not survive." But really accepting it and watching it happen are worlds apart from mere words. He is so precious. I'm not anywhere near ready to let him go.

A few days before Christmas our doctors started to hint to us Jarrott might not survive. They told us that every day he didn't progress made the chances of his survival a little less likely. Every day I hoped and prayed for some type of positive report, something good and healthy, a turn for the better. It wasn't happening.

As I grew more and more attached to Jarrott over these months—holding him, singing to him, caring for him as much as I could—the possibility of losing him became intolerable. I loved this child! He'd lie in his little crib, all hooked up to tubes and wires and monitors. And he'd look at me with such love and trust in his eyes. His big brown eyes would just sparkle. Even though he was so limited with all the medical paraphernalia, his spunky personality shone out of those wonderful eyes.

He had several favorite nurses, and we could tell he was happier and rested better when they were on duty. One in particular, Dorothy—a slim, beautiful Asian nurse in her mid-thirties—took the most meticulous care of him. He'd often get sores on his bottom from the excessive stooling due to his bowel not working right. With her shoulder-length black hair bouncing, Dorothy would sweep in and whip up a Jacuzzi bath. I laughed so hard the first time I saw it! She'd take a little pink tub, fill it with warm water and place Jarrott in it, covered with warm, wet washcloths. Then she'd run the oxygen tubing right into the water to blow bubbles on his bleeding bottom. The extra oxygen and warm water worked wonders on his sores. For Dorothy it was never an inconvenience or irritation to do extra things for Jarrott. He was her boy and he loved her.

She was off for several days before Christmas and when she came back in, he was so excited. He grinned at her as if to say, "Where in the world have you been?" The nursing staff adored Jarrott because he was so sweet and social. When he was feeling well, he loved having people in his room making over him and talking to him.

He was starting to interact and smile so appropriately. It was hard for me to wrap my mind around the doctors telling us he might not make it. They told us he could linger for up to six months and still succumb to the bronchopulminary dysplasia, or chronic lung disease.

As the doctors continued to talk to us—sometimes on a daily basis—about the possibility of Jarrott dying, I began to feel something in my spiritual life I had never experienced before. I started to feel angry at God. Really angry. I kept thinking back over my life...all the years I had lived for Him and been devoted to Him. I was a tiny girl when I first heard about Jesus. My family started going to the little Bible church down the road from our house, and God began to work on my parents' hearts. My dad was the first to understand Jesus had died on the cross for his sins and took the punishment my dad deserved. He recognized he needed to repent of his sins and make a complete turnaround in his life. But he knew he couldn't make the changes that needed to be made on his own. He asked Jesus Christ to come into his life and forgive him of his sins. And just like Christ rose from the dead to new life, He gave a new beginning to my dad. And our family began to change.

Later that year I was so privileged to have my mom explain my need for a Savior and lead me to Jesus. Soon our whole family had come to the Lord. I was so excited about knowing Jesus; I told everyone who would listen about Him. In fact, I almost got myself kicked out of preschool after I sat all the other children down and told them where they were going to go if they didn't accept Jesus.

When I made that commitment as a child, I had no concept of how that would affect my life later on. But my relationship with Christ became my foundation and determined who I became and how I would get through unfathomable trials as an adult.

In my anger, I thought about how I'd wanted to serve God and live for Him as far back as I could remember. From making wise decisions of purity in high school to studying Biblical studies in college and becoming a pastor's wife, I felt like I'd given God my very best. I'd given Him all and He was repaying that love and devotion with this! He was going to allow Jarrott to die and it wasn't fair. I was furious with Him.

This wasn't something I addressed or shared with anyone. Joel had no idea of the huge battle going on inside me. I'd go to the hospital every day and put my sweet "pastor's wife" face on. When people would ask how I was doing, I'd smile and say, "Fine. We're doing fine."

But inside I was a train wreck! Somewhere along the line I'd quit talking to God except to tell Him how mad I was and sometimes to beg for Jarrott's life. I vented a lot of things to Him in my anger. I wasn't reading the Bible much, I was simply ignoring Him except to tell Him how unfair and wrong He was to do this to me! It was not a time in my life I'm proud of. Maybe it was normal to question God and ask "why" and be angry. But that doesn't make it right. And I knew it. Not only was I angry, I was intensely miserable. God was my only real source of comfort. He was my hope, my rock and my stronghold. And the bottom line is, if I didn't have Him, I really had nothing at all. No hope at all. As horrible as those days were, it was a learning time for me that changed my life forever.

As I journaled, my handwriting often became sloppy and nearly unreadable as I anguished.

> We have prayed begged, pleaded, sobbed and groveled for a mighty miracle. But I don't think He's going to do it this time. Why not? Why not this time? My heart rages with grief and agony and nameless other feelings. I KNOW God can heal! I KNOW He performs miracles. We've heard stories, seen it in other's lives. WHY NOT OURS?

Many times I thought I would explode in my grief and anger. Modern psychology might have told me to scream and vent my anger, but what I really needed was a renewed relationship and fellowship with my God.

In all of my anger and my asking "why," God was still incredibly patient with me. Although I wasn't spending time in His Word, as I should have been, He was faithful to continue to bring Scripture to my mind. The particular day He broke through my anger and I surrendered to Him, He reminded me of Romans 8:28. This was a verse I'd known and memorized since I was a child. It was a verse I'd taken for granted many times. But the beautiful words struck a chord in me that day and I've never looked at this verse the same.

"And we know that in all things God works for the good of those who love Him, who have been called according to His purpose."

"And we KNOW." I had to stop right there for some serious contemplation. It didn't say "and we think" or "and we hope." We can know for certain all things, *everything*, every single thing will work for the good of those who love Him. I had to look long and hard into my heart. Did I love Him? Really, truly love Him? I knew I did. I had loved Him for most of my life. Was I called to His purpose? Yes, again I knew I was. Something solidified for me at this point. Either God's Word is true, or it's not. And if it's not true, I have no hope at all. But if it is true, and I believe with my whole heart that it is, then I had to believe and trust Romans 8:28 is true as well. And if Romans 8:28 is true, then God was working out Jarrott's life and even possibly his death for good.

It wasn't an overnight process. It took time for me to revive my relationship with the Lord. And at times I'd still find myself getting angry and going back to the "why" question. These were times it was really important for me to remember the faithful followers of God in Scripture who had endured with grace and strength trials far more difficult than mine. Such as Joseph, whose life had impacted me deeply as a young person. When I look at his life, I think if anyone in history had a right to be mad and bitter, it would have been Joseph. Sold as a slave, left to die....not by his enemies, but by his brothers! However, I don't think for one minute Joseph had an angry, bitter heart. Because God blessed

Josephs' life. I don't think God would have blessed him so abundantly if he had hatred and anger concealed in his heart toward his brothers. Joseph had learned to forgive. And beyond that, he'd learned to find contentment and peace in his circumstances. God was enough for Joseph.

The apostle Paul was also an inspiration to me. I found it so fascinating to read his account in 2 Corinthians 11 about the times he was shipwrecked, beaten, stoned, hungry, thirsty and much more. I never read about him questioning or getting angry at God. And he was serving God with his whole life, with everything in him! In fact, a few books past Corinthians, he was sitting in a cold jail cell when he wrote the beautiful book of "joy," Philippians. In Philippians 4:11 he even states he'd learned to be content, no matter what! In sickness, whether well fed or hungry, rich or poor, Paul was content.

I certainly couldn't say that about my life! I wasn't content with my circumstances. I wasn't content with my trials and my suffering. But God was working on my heart, changing me, molding me slowly into a godly woman. What a challenge He had ahead of Him!

On Christmas Eve, after we'd been at the hospital and spent time with Jarrott, we let McKenzie open her little pile of gifts in our hotel room. She was so excited to have some new toys. We were hoping they'd keep her entertained during the long days at the hospital. My mom and dad volunteered to have the kids in their room that night so that was the best gift Joel and I could have received! It had been a long time since we'd had a full night's sleep without Brennan's monitors going off all night. We had a bottle of flavored iced tea and someone had given us some little fancy glasses. We turned on the Christmas music in our room and spent some much needed time relaxing and enjoying each other's company. It was so hard to put the stress of our situation out of our minds, but for a few hours that night God gave us the gift of laughter and quiet time together.

Christmas morning held a surprise for us I still haven't figured out. We woke up to a beautiful, crisp Christmas day and got ready to go to the hospital. When we went downstairs to the lobby very early that morning, a basket was waiting for us. I still have the little gift card that read, "To the Millermon Family from Santa." That big basket was full of all kinds of goodies for us—toys for the kids and little gifts for Joel and me, along with fresh-baked cookies. We only knew a few people in the Denver area and they all lived a long ways away. I never did find out who brought that basket to us, but God used them in a great way that morning to encourage our hearts. It's amazing how such a small thing brought a smile to us. It made us feel so good that someone cared and put thought and effort into doing something so special for our family.

When I get the opportunity to speak to women's groups at conferences or retreats, I spend significant time in my sessions teaching about how to get through trials successfully. We all go through difficulties—it's a fact of life, so we need to learn to do it right! Sometimes the things I teach are from mistakes I've made and have learned from. But one of my favorite things to share is how to have a sensitive, servant's heart to others who are going through trials. I have realized that if I'm willing, I can be used by God to bring comfort and encouragement to other people's lives because of what I have lived through and endured.

I love the verses Paul wrote in 2 Corinthians 1:3-4 because they give me so much hope, knowing my trials are not in vain. He says, *"Praise be to the God and Father of our Lord Jesus Christ, the Father of compassion and the God of all comfort. Who comforts us in all our troubles, so that we can comfort those in any trouble with the comfort we ourselves have received from God."*

Those verses are so good for my heart! The trials I go through and the things that are overwhelming and threaten to destroy me can be used for God's glory. But so much of that depends on me. Am I willing to be used? Am I responding with the right attitude to what God allows into my life? Sadly, I can't always say that is the case.

I read a book not long ago that completely changed my thoughts on being a servant. I've always known that as a Christian I'm a servant of God, but I didn't grasp the full meaning of that truth. In Chuck Swindoll's book, *Improving Your Serve*, he states two truths that changed the way I was thinking about my trials. The first one is this:

"Nothing touches me that has not passed through the hands of my heavenly Father. Nothing."

Wow! What a wonderful concept! When I first read that quote, my eyes filled with tears as I pictured my trials slipping through the very loving hands of my heavenly Father. Nothing surprised Him. He knew far in advance what I would go through and how much I could bear. He never gave me too much or failed to give me the strength to bear up under the stress. He remains faithful every day.

The second quote that Chuck Swindoll claims in the midst of trials is this:

"Everything I endure is designed to prepare me for serving others more effectively. Everything."

Again, a completely hope-filled statement. When I allow God to mold me and work in me, He can design me into someone He can use as a tool to serve others. I may not know the answer to the "why" question I ask so many times when things seem insurmountable in my life. But I do know this; when I suffer, I will be comforted by a loving God who will in turn use me to comfort others with the comfort I've received from Him. It's hard to forget it's not all about me! I'm part of a bigger picture and God can use me greatly, even in my suffering, if I'm willing. I'll have the depth and compassion needed to comfort others in need because of what I've survived and learned. I often have to reevaluate if I'm being faithful to use the experiences and lessons God has entrusted to me.

Am I being faithful to serve? The thoughtful person, who left that basket for us on Christmas morning, may never know the impact they had on our hearts. But they were faithful to serve and meet a need. Their kind act was truly a blessing to us especially as we were heading into the most difficult part of our journey.

Coming Home
By Ginger Millermon
© *Anothen Music 2002*

My tears are flowing freely now
My heart just breaks in two
I whisper Your name down on my knees
Lord, I'm coming home to You
I'm coming home to You…

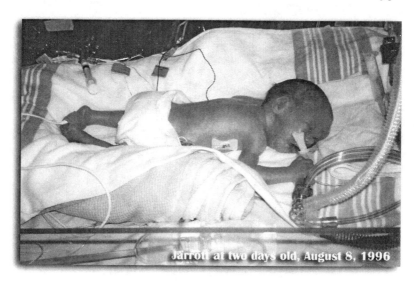

Jarrott at two days old, August 8, 1996

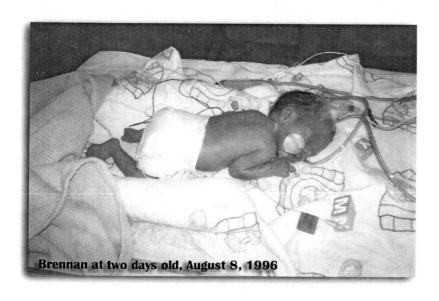

Brennan at two days old, August 8, 1996

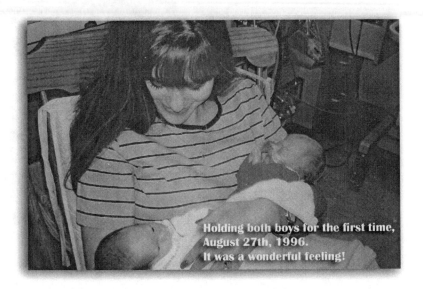

Holding both boys for the first time,
August 27th, 1996.
It was a wonderful feeling!

At one month old, we still had no idea the
ordeal we were facing in the coming days.

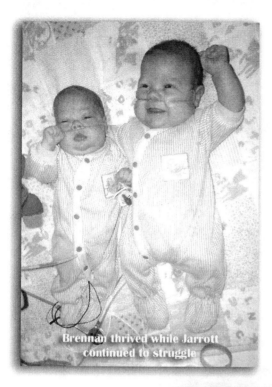

Brennan thrived while Jarrott
continued to struggle

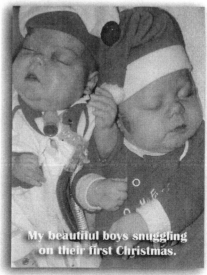

My beautiful boys snuggling
on their first Christmas.

McKenzie loved holding Brennan.

She brought a lot of laughter
during a very dark time.

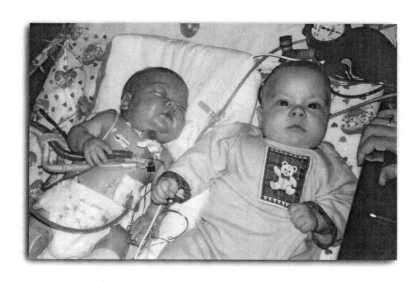

Trying to figure out
how to say good-bye.

Treasuring every moment with Jarrott when he was in a coma.

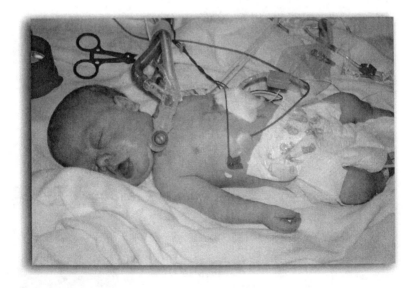

Chapter Eight

December 1996

OVER THE CHRISTMAS HOLIDAY, while my parents were still visiting, my mom made this profound statement one morning. "You guys are stressed out."

I was confident that comment could have taken some kind of prize for understatement of the year! But she was right. We were exhausted, worn down and stressed out. Mom's solution for us a couple days after Christmas was that we needed a date. It had been a *long* time since Joel and I had been on any type of a date, so that sounded good to us! In fact, I think the last date we'd gone on, we'd wrecked the car. So I got all fixed up, with growing excitement, about having dinner out and a nice, relaxing evening with my husband. Mom watched McKenzie and Brennan and took turns with my dad sitting with Jarrott at the hospital.

We weren't sure where we were going that night, but dinner was first priority on the agenda. We drove around Denver looking for a fun place to eat and ended up in some parking lot. I don't even remember where. After all of our good intentions, by the time we reached a destination, we were too exhausted to even make a move for the door. We were so tired. Spiritually, mentally, physically, we were at the end of our resources. I looked into Joel's eyes that night and was surprised to see they were full of tears. That was out of the ordinary for him. I felt my tears start the instant I saw his.

"I'm so scared," he whispered, his voice breaking. "He's not going to make it."

My tears started in earnest then. "I know," I cried. I crawled out of my seat in our minivan and right into Joel's lap, wrapping my arms around his neck. We sat in that cold parking lot, somewhere in Denver, holding each other tight and sobbing our hearts out. And then we began to pray.

"Lord," I started brokenly, "we love this child. We want him to be in our family, to be part of our lives. We want to take him home. Please, God." Moments passed before I could continue. And then I prayed some of the hardest words I have ever uttered. "But God, if that's not what You want for us, if that's not Your plan for our family, we really want what You want more than what we want."

I'm not sure if there is a more difficult thing for a parent to do. Completely surrendering your child into God's hands, and really meaning it. Opening up a tight fist that is clinging to hope and letting it go. Wanting His will more than my own.

Our broken pleas continued. "God, if You're going to take Jarrott home, please do it quickly. Please just take him and don't let him suffer any longer. Oh, God, that's not what we want, but if that's what You're going to do, just take him home."

As our doctors had been talking to us over the previous weeks, we understood Jarrott could linger for many months and die a slow, agonizing death. As much as we wanted him to survive, we'd come to a place of surrendering Jarrott and being willing for God to take him home.

Instead of being a romantic date that night, December 28, 1996 was much more significant. It proved to be a turning point in both Joel and my acceptance of God's will in Jarrott's life and in our family.

On New Year's Eve, Joel and I walked into the nursery early in the morning as we did every day—anxious to see how Jarrott had fared through the night. My parents had gone home and McKenzie was staying with Joel's parents in Paonia for a few days. We pushed Brennan with us in a stroller with his monitors and oxygen. Jarrott's doctors quickly pulled us aside.

Overnight, Jarrott had evidently contracted some type of virus. That was the only thing they could attribute to the severe and dramatic decline in his condition. His carbon dioxide level was extremely high. A normal range was 35-45 and his levels had soared over 120. The doctors sedated Jarrott and put him on Pavulon, a medication that would temporarily paralyze him to try to bring the extreme carbon dioxide level down. They were hoping the ventilator would be more effective pulling the deadly gas from his lungs if he were paralyzed, not fighting against the ventilator. They solemnly informed us this was the last intervention they could do to try to save his life.

Over the next several days, we rarely left the hospital as we waited for some sign to indicate the medications were working and he was starting to recover. But his situation remained very volatile and unstable. His carbon dioxide level stayed dangerously high even as they maxed out his medications and ventilator settings. He was unaware of his surroundings, as he lay paralyzed in a drug-induced coma with the ventilator breathing every breath for him.

After three days, tests were run that showed devastating lung and airway disease. The more oxygen and ventilation he required to stay alive, the more damage was being done to his fragile lungs. It was a vicious cycle for him. His airways were floppy and collapsible, clamping down easily and quickly. The doctors worked tirelessly on him for several days and then called us in for a care conference.

I will never forget walking into that conference room. All of Jarrott's doctors, specialists and several of his nurses—his team devoted to his care—were present. They were all seated around a big oval table in the center of the conference room, and as Joel and I walked into the room I looked into each of their eyes. My heart sank as I saw their tears. I knew this was it. The medications weren't working. We were going to lose him.

The head neonatologist spoke up first. With short brown hair and wire-rimmed glasses, she was in her early fifties and had been quiet and hard to read through most of our time there. To be honest, she hadn't been my favorite doctor to deal with and we'd struggled to connect with her, as her answers to our questions were often somewhat evasive and uninformative. However, this day the compassion in her voice was clear and it was very evident she was grieving with us.

"We have fought so hard for Jarrott." She shook her head, in tears. "And he is *such* a fighter. But it's not working. We have tried everything and there is nothing left for us to do. We need to gradually wean him off of this medication and when we do that, his carbon dioxide level is going to get even higher. It's very possible his lungs will collapse and he will not be able to breathe, even on the ventilator. At some point, as his carbon dioxide level rises, he will slip into a coma and pass away."

The room was silent for several minutes as the doctors allowed Joel and me to take this in. The tears were streaming freely down our faces and some of the dedicated nurses who had cared for him so selflessly also struggled to regain composure.

When we were finally able to speak and ask questions, we directed several to the pulmonologist.

Joel started first, "What about a heart-lung transplant? Would that be an option?" We had been told irreparable damage to his heart was happening as he struggled so hard to breathe.

The pulmonologist shook his head. "He would never survive that. Even if a transplant was available and an option, he would never even make it through surgery. He is far too weak."

I braved the next question. "What if, somehow, he survived the next few days? If this virus leaves his system and he makes it through the week. What are his chances long-term?" My voice broke. "Just to be able to bring him home and have him in our family. Please don't sugarcoat it. We need to hear the truth." Several times we'd felt we weren't getting all the information we wanted and needed.

Again, the pulmonologist shook his head. "It would take a miracle," he replied matter of factly. "This child cannot live with these lungs. They are black with disease."

He continued. "And honestly, if by some miracle he survives, he will have no quality of life. He may never walk, he will probably never talk as he will most likely remain trached on a ventilator. He'll most likely be in a wheelchair for the rest of his life with very severe cerebral palsy. He will have no quality of life."

Time stood still. Quality of life. Those words jumped out to us. We'd not really heard anything this specific on Jarrott's prognosis long-term. Or perhaps we had, but this was the first time it really sank in. That if somehow Jarrott survived, he would not lead anything close to a normal life. It wouldn't be simply a few years on the trach and ventilator and feeding tube and then he'd be fine. It wasn't going to happen. He would not be going to school with Brennan, playing football and riding bikes on a sunny day. He would be relegated to a wheelchair, unable to walk or talk or do anything. Joel and I both sat speechless in our grief.

Moments of silence passed before the neonatologist spoke up again. "You do have one other option today."

I felt a small spark of hope. "What is it? What can we try?"

She paused. "Well, you can take him off of the ventilator and let him go now. He is going to die. If you take him off life support while he's still paralyzed and sedated, it will be over for him very quickly. He will not feel any pain and it will be over for you as well. You've been through so much. You need to be able to get back to a normal life for your other children."

Joel and I looked around the room to see the response of the other doctors. Most nodded in agreement.

We had questions we needed answered. "Does he still have brain activity? Is he brain dead now after all he's been through?" We truly didn't know at this point.

She hesitated, thoughtful. "No, he's not brain dead. Our latest scans show there is still brain activity. But you have to understand, he cannot survive. This is the easiest and best thing for both him and your family."

Joel and I looked at each other briefly, each of us feeling the pressure of the decision Jarrott's doctors wanted us to make.

We'd prayed about this—prayed long and hard we'd never have to make this decision. It didn't take long to decide. "We have to wait. We're going to wait and pray for a miracle. We won't cut God's hand short."

The doctors reluctantly accepted our decision, although we knew they disagreed with us. It was sobering and more than a little intimidating, standing firm, even though we knew we were going against our doctors' advice and opinions. We felt as if suddenly we were in a battle for Jarrott's life. Although we knew the chances of his survival were small, we wanted to give him every possible chance to live.

As we left the conference room that day, we understood what would transpire over the next several days. As they weaned the medications out of Jarrott's body, the carbon dioxide would reach a lethal level, his vital organs would be damaged and shut down, and he'd pass away. Walking down the cold, long corridors of Children's Hospital that day, I felt grief hit me full force. I was the mother of a dying child. My son lay dying and there was absolutely nothing I could do to help him, nothing I could do to stop it. It was the most helpless feeling in the world. I leaned against Joel and wept as we made our way back to Jarrott's room.

We were all alone in Denver. We really didn't know anyone there. One or two local pastors had visited over the weeks and we were getting acquainted with some of the Fellowship of Christian Athlete staff. But we had no one we were close to, no one we could call who would rush to our side. My family had gone home to Kansas and Joel's family was hours away on the other side of the mountains.

There are times when you need someone to cry with, to pray with you, to comfort you. This was one of those times for us. Joel and I were both so grief stricken and broken, not sure where to turn. I will never cease to be grateful for what God did that day. As we walked by the family waiting room, I happened to look up and glance in the door. There, sitting on one of the couches, was my youth leader from high school and his wife. Virgil and Sue Johnson had known me most of my life and been very instrumental in my years as a teenager. I swiped at my tears as Joel and I hurried into the room.

"What are you doing here?" I was so surprised to see them. They were living in Nebraska and I hadn't seen them for years.

Virgil spoke up, "We were passing through Denver today and thought we'd try to see you. We've been praying for you and Jarrott and your family."

What a balm to my heart to sit down across from them and pour out our grief. They listened in tears as we told them Jarrott was dying. I don't remember a lot of what was said that day. I know they cried with us and prayed with us. And then Virgil shared something that would be a tremendous comfort to me in the ensuing days. He opened his Bible, and he read the first part of one simple verse.

Psalm 46:10—"Be still and know that I am God…"

Oh, how I needed to hear that…to just be still and know that God would be sovereign. That He would be good and do the best thing for our family. The decisions we were being pressured to make weren't ours to make at all. God was in control and we could trust Him and wait on Him.

Their visit with us was short, but affected us profoundly. That God would make sure someone was right there when we needed them most continues to be incredible to me. That the Johnson family would "happen" to be driving through Denver the very hour of our difficult care conference was much more than an amazing coincidence. It was God's faithfulness and grace being poured out once again in our lives.

As the weaning of medication and the waiting began that day, I once again filled the pages of my journal with my grief as I struggled to understand and cope with our imminent loss.

January 3, 1997

I don't even know where to start. I have so many feelings and thoughts surging through me every hour. I think I could fill this book.

Jarrott is very, very sick now. Just a few days back, on December 28, Joel and I asked God that if He was going to take Jarrott, He would do it quickly. It seems He's going to answer this prayer.

We have trusted, prayed, hoped and prayed some more. We've tried to be good, loving parents. I know that we would raise this child up to be a man of God, a man after God's own heart to the best of our ability. Why can't we have that opportunity? My heart is screaming in pain to know why.

We have been grieving for days...will continue to grieve. Sometimes it's overwhelming. The pain is more than emotional. It's physical, spiritual, mental. We love this child. We have struggled with him, cheered him on, hoped for him dreamed for him. Oh God, please. Please spare my baby. We know that nothing will spare him other than a miracle. I've asked so many times and yet I ask again. I can do no less. As a parent, as a believer in Your might and power. I must ask again.

"Be still and know that I am God."
I know, Lord. I know You're holy, just, and sovereign. I know You have a good, pure and perfect reason for our trials, for Jarrott's struggles and possibly even his death. I don't have to know why. I don't have to know how or when. I just have to trust.

My heart longs to just be still and know You are God.

The time had come for me to put into action all the things I'd gleaned over the years in my Christian walk. I'd discipled others and assured many that God would be faithful in any circumstance. All pretense was stripped away as my soul was purified through the hottest fire of adversity. Was God present? Was He faithful in this moment? Even in my anguish, His comfort and presence surrounded me in a peace that measured beyond human comprehension.

Be Still
By Ginger Millermon
© *Anothen Music 2002*

...For Your mercies are new
At the dawn of every day
And I will not be consumed
If I'll get on my knees and pray
And be still
And know You are my God...

Chapter Nine

___

THE HARDEST PHONE CALLS we ever had to make came after our care conference. It was excruciating to call both sets of grandparents and tell them their grandson was dying. Our parents and my brother, Bob, and his family were soon on their way to Denver.

McKenzie came with Joel's parents and we struggled to know how to explain to a not-quite two-year-old that her brother wouldn't be with us any longer. She called him "Baby Jert" and loved to stand by his bed and grin at him. After trying to explain Jarrott would be leaving us, she cocked her curly-haired little head to one side and said, "Baby Jert goin' to heaven?" Oh, the simple, beautiful faith of a child!

When my parents arrived, they walked into the room and saw all the stuffed animals surrounding Jarrott's bed, as he lay oblivious in his coma. My dad was instantly overcome with the enormity of losing his tiny grandson and left the room to compose himself.

The doctors had moved Jarrott to an isolation room so

we'd have more privacy to tell him goodbye. Although he was still in a drug-induced coma as they slowly weaned the medications, Joel and I spent most of our time taking turns sitting in the big, green leather recliner in his room holding him. We didn't want to leave his side, knowing our time with him was limited and precious. As I look back on pictures from those days, the exhaustion and grief is clear in our eyes although we continued to try to smile for the camera. The smiles on our faces certainly did not reflect the sorrow in our hearts. One day in particular, Joel took a picture of me with my head on the bed, my face just inches from Jarrott's. I still can't look at that picture without tearing up, because I remember the suffocating anguish and impending loss I was feeling at that moment.

As our family arrived at the hospital, the staff compassionately reserved a small sitting room for our family and put a sign on the door so we wouldn't be interrupted as we grieved together. We spent time in Jarrott's hospital room in shifts. As we prayed over him and held him, we started talking about a Scripture passage in the book of James. James 5 is a beautiful chapter about persevering and having patience in suffering. It also addresses the need to keep the faith and pray in the midst of difficult circumstances. Verse fourteen held particular interest to us.

James 5:14 says, *"Is any one of you sick? He should call the elders of the church to pray over him and anoint him with oil in the name of the Lord."*

This wasn't something either Joel or my family grew up practicing. And yet it seemed evident to all of us it should be done. Joel, Dad Millermon, and my dad were all elders in their churches. And so the afternoon everyone arrived, the men gathered around Jarrott's bed and anointed his tiny chest with oil, praying for healing for those diseased lungs. When it came Joel's turn to pray, I have to say, I was a little surprised.

"Lord," he started reverently, "this really would be the perfect opportunity for You to show everyone what You can do. Everyone has given up on him, but I know You can heal him."

I guess I didn't think God needed Joel to remind Him this would be a good opportunity, but I sure did agree with him! What an amazing story we'd have to tell to give God glory if He allowed Jarrott to live. And it would clearly be all Him, because there was absolutely no other hope left.

It's a hard thing to explain, but although I knew God *could* heal Jarrott, I didn't think it was His plan for our family. I never, not once, lost faith in God's abilities. But I had come to a place of recognizing God doesn't always answer the way we want Him to answer. He is sovereign. I was reminded often of Isaiah 55:8-9.

" 'For My thoughts are not your thoughts, neither are your ways My ways,' declares the Lord. 'As the heavens are higher than the earth, so are My ways higher than your ways and My thoughts than your thoughts.' "

I had finally come to a place of accepting the truth of those verses and felt an inexplicable peace in knowing it was out of our hands and completely in His. I had never known a person could grieve and have sorrow and peace all at the same time. But that's exactly the place I found myself.

January 3, 2007

As grieved and as anguished as we are, we have complete peace in Jarrott's eternal future. When he passes from this life, he will be in eternal peace with God.

"Safe in the arms of Jesus, safe on His gentle breast,

There by His love ore shaded,
sweetly my soul shall rest."

Jarrott has had very little time to rest in this
life. If he goes home, he will be at peace and
total rest in Jesus' loving arms. I envy him greatly
for the joy and beauty he will see ahead of us.

The doctors advised us we were facing our last day with Jarrott. They did not expect him to make it through the night. I asked Dad Millermon to call the funeral home in Paonia and make all the arrangements. He broke down more than once on the phone as he helped settle those plans. The funeral home director knew Joel and Dad, and since Joel was a pastor he offered to do the funeral at no expense. They were waiting on our call to come and get Jarrott's body. We planned the funeral together. The mood in the room was somber and it was almost a surreal conversation, but I didn't want to be burdened with planning his service later when I knew the grief would be overwhelming. We wanted that wonderful old Fanny Crosby hymn "Safe in the Arms of Jesus" to be sung by a close friend, and planned for several of Jarrott's uncles to carry his casket. Dad Millermon was asked to preach, but thought it would be too difficult. We understood and asked my pastor from my home church in Kansas to do the service.

At some point during that time, the doctors told us where the morgue was and told me I could hold Jarrott as long as I needed to once he was gone. We were as prepared as parents can possibly be to tell a child goodbye. I don't think you can ever be totally ready for that, but the hospital staff was kind and accommodating, giving us plenty of time and privacy to grieve.

I laid Brennan in bed to nap with Jarrott several times so I could take pictures of the boys together. I wanted Brennan to always know how special and wonderful it was that he had a twin. Jarrott always loved to snuggle up with Brennan. Although he was in a coma, I hoped he'd feel Brennan's nearness as he cuddled close.

As we waited by his bed, I journaled one last prayer. Instead of being another plea for his life, I'd reached a point of thankfulness for the time we'd shared with this amazing little fighter.

> Thank you so much, Father, for the time we've had with this precious child. He has inspired us to hope beyond all hope, to trust You, and has blessed us in so many ways. Thank You for letting us have him. We have loved him with all of our hearts and have cared for him the best that we knew how. He is a priceless treasure from You.
>
> May Your will be done.

Over the following hours, the medications slowly weaned from his body, and he started to move for the first time since the Pavulon had paralyzed him. There was little change at first in his condition, and one of the nurses told us he could go on for weeks or months in the state he was in and still pass away. Although we were sickened to think of him lingering for months in that condition and still dying, we stood firm in our decision to keep him on life support.

Sunday after the New Year came and went with little change as the medications slowly wore off. His medical team was constantly monitoring him and was sending blood work to the lab to check his carbon dioxide level. We waited with dread, knowing the doctors expected his carbon dioxide to rise as the medications wore off.

And then Monday, January the 6th dawned. It was the boys' five-month birthday. Joel and I were standing beside the nurse's station that morning, asking some questions and talking about Jarrott's care. Blood work had again been sent to the lab that morning and when the fax machine started up, my heart sank. I assumed it was Jarrott's report and I simply did not want to see it. I continued to cling to a fragment of hope and I didn't want the lab results to shatter that fragile thread.

Our nurse pulled the sheet from the fax machine and confirmed it was Jarrott's lab work. Joel and I waited silently, our hearts pounding. Normally the nurses read off the results to us, but this time she handed the paper to us. We were very good at reading these reports by now. A long list of numbers signified different lab results on the page, but our eyes were only looking for the CO_2—the carbon dioxide level.

I held my breath as I searched for the number, and then I gasped! I couldn't believe my eyes. It was 55. His carbon dioxide was the lowest it had been in his entire life. Joel found the number at the same time I did and my eyes flew to his. We both instantly grinned. He was going to make it. We knew it. He was going to live and it was clearly God's intervention. There was no other explanation.

Our doctors were astounded and skeptical at the same time. More than once they warned us the body does strange things and most likely it was a fluke. They were convinced his carbon dioxide level would still go back up and he'd die. We were told his lungs would never heal enough for him to live. They cautioned us over and over not to get our hopes up, but we couldn't help it. Hope once again reigned in our hearts.

We had a wonderful nurse practitioner named Donna. In her late-thirties with beautiful red hair, she was very attached to Jarrott and was meticulous about his care. She'd taken off several days after the New Year and when she left, Jarrott was dying. She got the shock of her life when she came back to work and he was smiling at her.

Her first morning back, she was charting outside his room when we arrived. Her eyes were red and bloodshot and she looked exhausted. When she saw us, she instantly teared up.

"Guys, I went out drinking last night because I knew when I came into work this morning, his room would be empty. And I didn't know how to handle that." She blinked away tears.

"He was at the gate and someone said go back." She rolled her eyes at us with a smile. "Whatever it is you guys are praising or praying or whatever it is you're doing, you'd better keep it up! Because it's not over yet. He is not out of the woods and he has a long road ahead of him."

Donna was right. It was by no means over for us and Jarrott did have a very long road ahead of him. But it was the beginning of a healing process that would go on for years. I'm still astounded that we were literally waiting for Jarrott to die, and with no hope left and the funeral planned, God healed him. I know there is no way we can fathom the mind of God, but sometimes I think He must have let us do all we could as parents, let the doctors do all they could do in the medical field, and then God said, "Let me show you what I can do!"

Believe me—whenever I get the opportunity to share, I want to remind hurting hearts that there is nothing too big for God! No failing marriage, job situation, financial crisis or health issue is too much for Him. He is the God of the impossible. I have seen His power firsthand and am still in awe of how great He is. Romans 15:13 truly is a beautiful verse to me:

"May the God of hope fill you with all joy and peace as you trust in Him, so that you may overflow with hope by the power of the Holy Spirit."

God is not one bit hampered by predictions or statistics. He is totally in control and He is the God of hope.

Your Majesty is Everywhere
By Paul Marino and Ginger Millermon
2007 Van Ness Press, Inc. (ASCAP)/McKinney
Music, Inc. (BMI) (both admin. by LifeWay Worship Music Group).
All rights reserved. Used by permission.

All creation lifts its praise
To the greatness of Your name
In the whisper of the wind
And the fury of the seas
The beauty of the heavens
All declare
Your majesty is everywhere
And everywhere I look I see
Your majesty…

*"For You created my inmost being;
You knit me together in my mother's womb.
I praise You because I am fearfully and
wonderfully made; Your works are
wonderful, I know that full well."*

—Psalm 139:13-14

Part III

Chapter Ten

———

Now, I know what some of you are thinking. I've heard your stories and I've seen your tears as we've traveled all across this country sharing our story in concerts and conferences.

Sometimes God says no.

It's hard, it's not what we want, but it's true. Sometimes for our good and for His glory, God's answer is not what we wanted it to be. Even after the amazing miracle of Jarrott's survival, we saw this firsthand in our family.

In April of 1999, Joel's brother and sister-in-law, Steve and Melissa, were excited to be expecting the second set of Millermon twins. However, halfway into the pregnancy, they discovered something seriously wrong with one of the babies. They wouldn't know the extent of the problem until their births. We'd all been praying and waiting.

Adam and Abigail Millermon arrived six weeks premature and close to four pounds each. Abby was immediately swept away by doctors at her birth. She'd been born with underdeveloped intestines and underwent surgery within twenty-four hours.

Although Abby's issues were different from Jarrott's, we couldn't help but feel the similarities. Steve and Melissa were living in Grand Junction and the doctors knew that with Melissa's preterm labor and the complications one of the babies was facing, she needed to be in Denver. So they were flown to Denver, like us, hundreds of miles from home. They also had two young children at home to think about and find care for.

Adam thrived while Abby struggled. She was fed intravenously and the doctors worked tirelessly to find a way to keep her alive without the full function of her intestines. Although she endured great pain, Abby was a precious, beautiful baby girl who loved to hear her daddy's soothing voice and her mommy singing to her.

Three months and three days after her birth, on August 3, 1999, Abby went home to be with Jesus.

To be honest, I couldn't believe it. I thought for sure God was going to do the same miraculous thing in Steve and Melissa's family as he had in ours. We'd have two incredible stories to tell. I struggled with some guilt that God had spared Jarrott, but not Abby. Why did He do that? I don't know all the answers—in fact, I know very few in the scheme of things. But I do know that God is sovereign. And I have discovered sometimes I can't truly fathom God's sovereignty until I experience this kind of pain and am at the end of my rope.

So how do I deal with the disappointment in God's answer? I have to remember God is never taken by surprise at my trials. He is completely in control. Nothing slips by Him. Nothing is too small for Him to notice and too big for Him to solve. I also have to rely on the fact that God is good. No circumstance in my life changes that reality. God is immutable. He does not change. He is and always will be good.

I visited with a young widow recently about the loss of her husband and how she was handling it. I was moved by what she tells her three children often.

"God is good." She says, "Period. There is no 'but' after that phrase. God is good." I greatly admire this godly woman's faith.

Not long ago I asked Melissa, Abby's mommy, what got her through Abby's death. "Psalm 139:13-17," she said immediately. "It was Abby's story." Then she quoted it to me:

> "For You created my inmost being; You knit me together in my mother's womb. I praise You because I am fearfully and wonderfully made; Your works are wonderful, I know that full well.
>
> "My frame was not hidden from you when I was made in the secret place. When I was woven together in the depths of the earth, Your eyes saw my unformed body. All the days ordained for me were written in Your book before one of them came to be.
>
> "How precious to me are Your thoughts, O God! How vast is the sum of them!"

I fought back tears as she quoted those beautiful words, because they *were* Abby's story. Even as she was being formed in Melissa's womb, God knew her every part, her tiny frame and unformed body. He also knew exactly how many days she would spend on this earth. And in three short months, Abigail Millermon reminded us of God's sovereignty, goodness and holiness.

When my heart is breaking with unanswered questions, I go to the Psalms. Sometimes they are Psalms of triumphant praise, other times they are desperate laments, crying out to God for help. I lived in that book during the months Jarrott was in the hospital. Although his survival was miraculous, his road to recovery was slow. Many tears and many trials loomed ahead.

The long-term prognosis did not change and we were more than a little irritated when his doctors made comments such as, "Well, he'll never run a marathon, that's for sure." Or, "He won't be playing sports with those lungs." Sometimes I wanted to scream, "How do you know? Don't put limits on him already!" While I was determined not to take those comments to heart, deep down I wondered if their predictions for Jarrott's life would all come true.

The severity of lung disease and the possibility of brain injury from oxygen deprivation still loomed over us. One snowy day in January, not long after he started to improve, I was walking back to the St. Christopher House from the hospital. It had been a very hard day and the reality that Jarrott would not have a normal healthy life had been presented to me once again. While I continued to be incredibly thankful that Jarrott's life had been spared, the enormity of caring for a child with needs as complicated as Jarrott's seemed staggering.

As I stood shivering on the street corner in the falling snow, waiting for the light to change, tears streamed down my face as I thought, "He'll never grow up and get married. It will be so hard on him, being in a wheelchair his whole life. What will he be able to do? Who will love him and help him if I'm not there?"

Any parent of a special needs child knows what I mean when I say you have the "death of a dream." We have all these expectations for our children. Sometimes we want their childhood and life to look exactly like ours and other times we want them to have so much more than we had. But we have dreams and goals for them and when we realize it's not going to happen the way we'd hoped, there is a grieving process. I found myself having to work through that process many times.

When I'd get discouraged at the negative prognosis, Joel would always be very quick to remind me of what we'd already been through and that God wasn't finished with Jarrott. I had seasons when I needed many reminders. But no matter how dark the days would seem at times, we were immensely thankful we had not cut Jarrott's life short by taking him off of life support. The term "quality of life" haunted us as we realized the same issue we faced with Jarrott—being asked to let him go because of the difficult conditions he'd live with—was the same issue we confront in our society. It is the sanctity and the cherishing of every human life. Each one, each life, is precious in God's eyes. How can one person decide if another person's life will have enough "quality" that they should be allowed to live? I quickly became a passionate soul for the rights of unborn babies and those afflicted with special needs who can't speak up for themselves.

I have learned much on this journey. It has changed me. It has emboldened me and refined me. Trials often reveal the depth and maturity of our faith. As I look back, I clearly see how my faith has grown and deepened through the valleys. Although I tremble to think of going through such a trial again, I'm so thankful for the fruit that has grown in my life and in our family. God truly has been good.

Beautiful Place
(Abby's Lullaby)
By Ginger Millermon
© *Anothen Music 1999*

In Jesus' loving arms
He's holding you near
In a place of no pain and no tears
With angels singing praise to the King
And with a smile on your face
You hold tight to Jesus tender hand
In Your new heavenly place
Such a beautiful place

Chapter Eleven

February 1997

WITHIN TWO WEEKS OF his miraculous turn around, Jarrott was steadily progressing. He was significantly down on his oxygen needs and ventilator settings. They were working toward getting him on a portable ventilator so he could be transferred back to St. Mary's Hospital in Grand Junction, only seventy miles from home instead of hundreds of miles! I couldn't wait.

On February 21, 1997, Jarrott was finally stable enough to be flown back over the mountains to Grand Junction. It had been 117 days since Jarrott had been admitted to Children's Hospital in Denver. I had only been home twice in those months and it was a dream come true to be heading closer to home.

Life by no means returned to normal when Jarrott arrived at St. Mary's, but it did seem more tolerable. The hospital was still over an hour drive from home so I'd often stay with friends or family in Grand Junction, spend several days with Jarrott and then go home for a day or two. It wasn't ideal, but

I did get to spend more time with Joel, Brennan, and McKenzie. Joel's parent's continued to be an incredible help with the kids and meals. Brennan was finally off of his breathing treatments, monitors and oxygen and was much happier being in a more stable environment.

After we'd been home for a few weeks, Joel and I both came down with a stomach virus. We couldn't take a chance of giving it to Jarrott, so we were staying away from the NICU for a few days. Any type if illness could derail his healing. Jarrott was doing amazingly well and was making great developmental and physical progress. He was finally growing and since he was on steroids long-term, his face was swollen and round, but he was gaining some healthy weight as well. It was tremendously encouraging for us to see him laughing and smiling. His laugh was silent, as he was trached and couldn't make any noise, but it was fun to see his chubby little body shake with a giggle.

So we were shocked when we got a call in the middle of the night from the hospital while we were recovering from the flu. Jarrott's trach had plugged and when one of the respiratory therapists checked on him, he wasn't breathing. They rushed to change his trach tube, but by the time they got that done he had no heartbeat. The doctors were unsure how long he was down, but they estimated he was without oxygen for several minutes. They administered Epinephrine and started CPR, eventually bringing him back. But they didn't think he'd survive through the night.

Joel and I were in the car within minutes, racing to Grand Junction. It was a clear winter night and the stars were brilliant as I stared out the car window with tears rolling, pleading with God. I could not believe we were facing his death again. Joel was driving as fast as our little car would go, trying to get there in time to say goodbye. About halfway into our trip, a police officer stopped us. It was three in the morning and Joel was driving over forty miles an hour over the speed limit. Thankfully, the officer was kind enough (after he threatened to throw Joel in jail!) to let us go, but the rest of the trip was excruciatingly slow. We didn't know if Jarrott would be alive when we arrived.

He was still hanging on when we finally made it to the NICU. But he was having severe seizures, and tremors shook his little body. The doctors didn't have to tell us damage had been done. Words truly can't express the anguish we felt this time around. I could not believe God had spared him at Children's Hospital just for us to lose him now. We were warned he most likely had severe brain damage from the episode. Any dreams we'd been hanging on to for him, seemed to dissolve.

But again, God had other plans for Jarrott. After twenty-four hours, the seizures stopped and within a few days the tremors ceased. An EEG showed no seizures and plenty of brain activity. We were encouraged. But after that episode, the doctors sat us down for a very difficult care conference. I still appreciate the honest, yet gentle way our doctors dealt with us as St. Mary's. They were always realistic, yet never gave up hope, even when things looked hopeless. They shared with us at that care conference that Jarrott would probably need to be hospitalized long-term, even two or more years. It was a horrid thing to hear. They explained to us he was not growing new lung tissue fast enough and the disease in his trachea and airways was not improving. His airways continued to be soft and floppy and he'd be in distress every time he didn't have full ventilator support. If his ventilator quit or any tubing became disconnected, it was an emergency. They went on to say his chest films looked like a seventy-year-old smoker with emphysema. His lungs were so diseased. Jarrott would not be coming home for a very long time.

This care conference led Joel and me to a tough decision. We both came to the conclusion it was not the best thing for us at that time to stay in ministry at the church in Paonia and also to be so far from Jarrott. It was too much. Joel needed to be in a job he could leave in the evenings and devote more time to our family, and I had to find a way to be at home more consistently with Brennan and McKenzie. Much prayer went into this decision, but soon after that meeting Joel resigned from the church and we made plans to move closer to the hospital. I think it was one of the wisest decisions we made. Although it was hard moving away from Paonia, Joel's parents, and our wonderful church family, we'd come to realize that someday, whenever Jarrott came home, the higher elevation in Paonia would not be good for him. We saw God's faithfulness, again, this time to the ministry in Paonia. We loved the teens we worked with and grieved that we had to leave them. However, Joel's younger sister Karen and her husband, Mike, had recently moved to Paonia and willingly stepped in to lead the youth group. It was a relief to us to know someone would care for the teens.

The stress on Joel and my relationship had grown over the weeks we spent caring for Jarrott and trying to figure out how to have a family life while we were hundreds of miles apart. We certainly had our times of being very close and communicating well, but the months of being in the hospital were starting to take their toll. Unbeknownst to our friends and most of our family, we'd been struggling in our marriage for several months.

We made the decision when we moved, to swallow our pride and get marital counseling. We knew we had to work through some things for our families' sake. We sought out a certified Christian counselor and told him our situation. We didn't have two nickels to rub together and couldn't begin to pay his normal fees, but he graciously worked with our finances, even during weeks we couldn't pay him at all. He'd drive more than an hour from his home to meet with us in our basement, never even requesting we pay for his gas. I still chuckle when I remember one of our first meetings. Our counselor drew a huge volcano with smoke billowing out the top on his whiteboard. Then he pointed at me.

"That's you," he said. "You are going to blow." Pretty accurate description. He was right. The stress in my life was ridiculous and I had some real issues with frustration, anger, and unrealistic expectations to work through as well. Joel had his own issues to work on, but since he's not writing this book I won't bother you with them. Needless to say, we both had changes to make, and God used that time in our lives to help us understand each other and love each other better. We still use the tools of communication and other marriage skills we learned from our months in counseling.

Our situation and need for counseling was certainly not unique. I have spoken with many parents of special needs children over the years. I've often found a common thread of strain and struggle running through these marriages. Having a special needs child or child in the hospital long-term takes its toll on a relationship. Actually, just having healthy toddlers is difficult. I always encourage families to get some counseling and reach out for help if it's needed. There is nothing shameful in asking for help. Joel and I watched other couples as their marriages dissolved in our months spent in the NICU. Again, we determined not to be a statistic and took measures to make sure healing could take place in our marriage.

Life took on a little more of a routine after we moved to Grand Junction and rented a little house a few minutes from the hospital. Joel started working nights at a grocery store and days in a nursing home. I tried my hand at selling skin care products from our home. We were doing whatever it took to get by! By the end of April, Joel had a full-time job at the nursing home as a speech therapy assistant, and Jarrott was steadily progressing.

In fact, our neonatologists, Dr. Warda and Dr. Olewnik, sat us down one morning, and Dr. Warda stated, "Well, Jarrott has once again made fools of us all!" Just when everyone had become resigned to him being in the hospital long-term, his lungs started growing and his airways began to harden and grow the cartilage they needed to stay open. Hope glowed on the horizon!

I'd like to say that Jarrott came home that spring, but he didn't. We'd set a home date, get things prepared, and then he'd get sick and decline. I shed many tears that summer as dates we'd set for him to be home came and went. It continued to be a rollercoaster of emotions, and it was two steps forward and then several steps back for months.

The process for him to come home was quite enormous. Home health nursing had to be set up and nurses trained. We had a difficult time even finding nurses who were qualified to care for such a medically dependent patient. Also, most of the nurses who were qualified weren't pediatric nurses and didn't feel comfortable caring for a small child with such great needs. Home medical equipment companies also had to be found and our home electrical supply had to be inspected to make sure it would support his ventilator and equipment. It was complicated and tedious and most of that process fell to me while Joel worked.

Toward the end of the summer I was spending most of my time at the hospital trying to learn every part of Jarrott's care. Although he'd come home with twenty-four hour nursing care, Joel and I still needed to know every detail of caring for a child with a tracheotomy on a ventilator. We learned how to change his trach tube, suction, bag and resuscitate him, do his feedings through his gastric tube in his tummy, and many other duties.

We'd hoped to be home for the boys' first birthday, but when August 6, 1997 rolled around, we were still in the hospital. I was so touched by the efforts of the hospital to make that day special for us. The media got word about Jarrott's story and sent news crews to his party. They were fascinated by the little boy who was celebrating his first birthday and had never even left the hospital. Jarrott grinned and charmed them all. He and Brennan both wore party hats and reveled in all the attention. Family, friends, and hospital staff gathered to celebrate the big day. We had cake and balloons and although Jarrott wasn't eating anything yet by mouth, Brennan more than made up for him on that! He sat next to Jarrott's wheelchair in his highchair and ate as much cake as he could get his hands on. It was really a blessing to have such a special day for the boys' first birthday.

When I finally went home that night, I couldn't help but remember the day one year earlier when God had blessed us with the boys. One whole year in the hospital. It seemed unreal. As wonderful as our day had been, I couldn't keep my heart from asking, *"How long, Lord. How much longer?"*

When dreams get torn
when faith is worn
by doubts and fears
when hopes disappear
there's nothing you can feel
that Jesus cannot heal…

Chapter Twelve

September 1997

JOURNAL ENTRY

...Jarrott is home! Unbelievable! He came home on August 30th and what a wonderful day it was! Life is terribly busy around here now. I got twenty-five phone calls and twelve people at my door in one day this week. Jarrott has a nurse here round the clock so there's not a lot of privacy.

We had the date set for his homecoming on August 29th. We were so excited! We got up and began getting ready that morning and then Dr. Olewnik called. He was sick! I was so crushed I couldn't think straight. I cried buckets. But by the next morning he was fine and came home that afternoon. It's been so exciting. He loves being home and is just thriving. Bren and Kenz think he's pretty neat too and have adjusted well.

So, we still don't have a normal life but Jarrott is HOME and for that we are very thankful.

His homecoming was a major event, and Jarrott's respiratory therapist and nurses accompanied him and Joel on the medical van transferring him home. It was a huge undertaking! We had his room all set up for him complete with enormous oxygen tanks and home ventilators. Jarrott came home on an LP10 home ventilator. He had one in his bedroom and one on his Kid Cart wheelchair. If one ventilator failed, we'd always have a backup. And if our electricity went out, the battery would last long enough to get him to a hospital. He came home still needing an incredible amount of pressure from the ventilator to keep his airways open. He needed a PEEP (positive end expiratory pressure) of 12, which is more than most critical babies need at their worst. The rings of cartilage in his airways still had not hardened and there was no guarantee they ever would. We simply had to make sure everything was in place at all times to keep positive air pumping into his airways.

Even with all of the medical equipment, it was a dream come true to have him home at last. I was so excited when the medical transfer team arrived and backed their huge van up the driveway. It took a large lift to lower his heavy wheelchair with oxygen tanks on each side. My heart was very full to see him being wheeled into the house to his own bedroom. It had been a long time in coming. Jarrott's eyes were huge taking it in and I wondered what he thought about it all. It was his first ride in a vehicle, his first trip anywhere, and the only thing familiar to him was our faces.

He'd only been home for a couple of hours, and he was barely settled in, when his gastric tube fell out of his stomach. I couldn't believe it! This had never occurred before and I was convinced we were going to have to call an ambulance to take him right back to the hospital. We didn't have a vehicle equipped to take him anywhere. We were working on getting a ramp installed in our van, but didn't have it yet. Transferring him in his fragile condition and with all his medical equipment was dangerous for him and complicated.

We called the NICU and spoke to Dr. Olewnik. She wasn't quite sure what we should do. She suggested I call Jarrott's surgeon. Unfortunately it was his day off, but his office understood our dilemma and gave me his cell phone number. He was hiking in the mountains with his family when I finally reached him.

"Hello," I said anxiously. "This is Ginger Millermon and Jarrott just came home today. We were getting him settled in and his g-tube fell out!" I knew he was going to come speeding back to Grand Junction and help us out!

"Well, I'm up on the Monument and won't be home for a while. Do you have an extra tube there?"

"Yes, we have one, but no one knows how to put it in. Dr. Olewnik told us to call you and our nurse has never done it."

"Well, it's really not that hard. I'll talk you through it. You can do it."

Was he kidding me? "You want *me* to do it?"

"Sure, you need to know how to do it anyway." I think he might have been smiling at this point.

I took a deep breath and dug a little deeper. I had no idea this was just the beginning of years spent learning how to take care of a medically dependent child. I was quite proud of myself after I changed out that g-tube. I even teased Dr. Olewnik the next time I saw her that I'd changed a g-tube before she had.

Having nurses in our home twenty-four hours a day became the next big hurdle to overcome and adjust to. It didn't feel like we ever had any privacy with someone always there with us. Thankfully, several of Jarrott's wonderful nurses from the hospital signed up with the home health agency because they wanted to continue to work with him. It was a tremendous blessing when we'd have someone who intimately knew his needs watching over him. For the new nurses coming in, Joel and I would train them step by step in Jarrott's care. After a while Joel came up with the brilliant idea of videotaping each step of Jarrott's care. I'm sure some of those nurses must have rolled their eyes, but we were ruthless about making them sit down and watch and understand that video! We'd come a long way with Jarrott and we weren't taking any chances. In fact, our respiratory therapist made a detailed video for the fire department and ambulance crews so they'd know how to bag Jarrott's airways open the right way. I was thrilled when the fire department sent some of their men to meet Jarrott so they'd be ready to help him if the need arose.

And it did! Not quite a month after Jarrott came home, we had our first scare. Joel had wheeled him into our living room on a Sunday afternoon to watch the Bronco football game. The nurse had gone back to Jarrott's room to get something when Joel glanced over and saw Jarrott's face was blue. His airway had collapsed. Joel grabbed the bag and mask off of the back of the wheelchair to bag him and the whole thing fell apart. Tubes and connections were coming apart all over the place as Jarrott gasped for air. Joel was yelling for the nurse and I was calling 911. Joel and the nurse frantically tried to get things hooked up to the oxygen to bag him. After several terrifying minutes, they were bagging his airways open and he was recovering. But we could have lost him right there in our living room. Although Jarrott was doing better by the time the ambulance arrived, he spent a couple of days back in the hospital for observation after that event.

That proved to be the first of many times emergency services were called to our home. They knew our address well before long. We resuscitated him more times than I can remember and almost lost him several times. We were never sure what each day would bring and the stress level in our home continued to soar. We had nursing services to coordinate, home medical equipment deliveries, therapists who came several times a week and doctors who made house calls. Our home was a constant hub of action around Jarrott. It was exhausting and disrupting for any kind of family life, but it was still better than being back in the hospital.

I remember with amusement one particular event when we had to call EMS. It was early November and our landlord had called and warned us we needed to turn off the water to our underground sprinklers before the temperatures went below freezing at night or the pipes would freeze. He'd told me to talk to the neighbor about how to turn them off. With all the activity in our house, we'd forgotten. Late that night, Jarrott crashed and we had to resuscitate him again and call 911. Two fire trucks and an ambulance lit up our quiet little street. By morning, he was fine and I had almost forgotten about it. It was sort of becoming routine. I was standing in our front yard trying to determine if our sprinklers had frozen. I didn't want to be in trouble with the landlord!

Our elderly neighbor shuffled into our yard while I was pondering the sprinklers. Before I even had a chance to ask him how to turn the water off, he spoke up, "So, you guys had some excitement last night, huh?

I sucked in a breath. "Oh, no! Did your sprinklers freeze?"

He looked entirely confused and I realized what he meant. "Oh! The fire trucks! Sorry. Yeah, we had to call EMS, but he's fine now." He must have really wondered about me. The sprinklers were fine.

McKenzie and Brennan did exceptionally well during all of this. They were so adaptable and swiftly adjusted to all the action. McKenzie was so social; she loved having the extra people around. In fact, we caught her several times sneaking out of bed and into Jarrott's room in the middle of the night to talk with the nurses. More than once I found her sitting on a nurse's lap, reading a book in the wee hours of the morning. It took a little extra discipline to convince her to stay in bed at night.

Again, we had the most amazing, compassionate doctors during this time. Early in his homecoming, Dr. Olewnik from St. Mary's came by to check on Jarrott and listen to his lungs. It was nearly impossible to get Jarrott out of the house. Eventually, we had a ramp put in our van and we could get his wheelchair in, but it wasn't the safest thing for him to be away from his home ventilator and a stable, predictable environment. Our pediatrician, Dr. Pacini, became a lifeline to us and made weekly house calls on his day off and any other time we needed him. Not only that, he and his wife, Lene, became dear friends and a big part of our support system.

One of our doctors at Children's Hospital had been a sweet young woman completing her internship in the NICU. In her early thirties, she was preparing to launch her career and had taken a keen interest in Jarrott. She always had a warm smile for us and we'd appreciated her input and support at Children's. Several months after Jarrott came home, she stopped by for a visit. She was in Grand Junction doing some shifts at St. Mary's and remembered our family and gave us a call, asking to come by to see Jarrott. By this time, Jarrott was on a longer set of tubing and was beginning to scoot around the house. Our nurses could barely keep up with him, pushing his enormous wheelchair behind him. It was great fun seeing the stunned look on her face when she laid eyes on Jarrott.

"I can't believe what I'm seeing! I know what we saw at Children's with Jarrott was a miracle. But this is even more incredible. I never thought he'd get out of his wheelchair." She sat down on our couch and asked us to fill her in on how he was progressing. After hearing our report she shook her head in amazement.

"I know no one told you this at Children's, but when he left the hospital, no one expected him to survive." She looked down. "We sent him home to die."

She left our home that day with a smile on her face and a promise to tell the rest of Jarrott's doctors in Denver how well he was doing. It was vastly important to us that they knew God was still working in Jarrott's life. That he was alive and thriving!

God also provided us with some wonderful nurses who were a blessing to us. Arla, Caprice, Kathy, Marilyn and Tanya became some of Jarrott's favorite nurses and over the months some of them basically became part of our family.

But as accommodating as everyone tried to be, it's not easy having someone live with you constantly and we had to get pretty creative to get any type of privacy. I chuckle, remembering how Joel and I tried to have a decent fight with a nurse sitting in the next room. We'd usually lock ourselves in our tiny bathroom. I'd sit on the edge of the tub and Joel would sit on the toilet and we'd whisper back and forth. We discovered it's really hard to have a good fight in a whisper. One time I even hired a babysitter so Joel and I could drive down the block and work a few things out.

Several weeks into our new home situation, one of our friends, who was also a nurse, recognized Joel and my need for a date. She called and volunteered to baby-sit McKenzie and Brennan so Joel and I could attend a Christian concert in town. It had been a long time since we'd been able to go anywhere together, so we were very grateful. We decided with two nurses in the house, surely they'd be okay for a few hours! It was a wonderful, refreshing evening of praise and worship we desperately needed.

Partway through the concert, a singing trio shared about their concern for children in third-world countries. Joel and I were both saddened and burdened by the overwhelming need. I was struck with the fact that, while I couldn't help them all, surely our family could at least help one child. I think our hearts were particularly tender since God had recently spared Jarrott's life. I wanted to help someone else's child live. I knew what it felt like to be the mother of a dying child and I didn't want any other mother, in any part of the world, to have to feel that pain.

That night we started to sponsor a little boy named Bukulo from Ethiopia, Africa, through a Christian humanitarian organization. Bukulo lived with his parents, who were farmers in a desperately poor region of Ethiopia. None of his family had ever been able to afford attending school so they were not literate or educated. It was a special privilege for us to know that by supporting Bukulo, we were helping his whole family and guaranteeing he'd be able to go to school. In the ten years now that we've sponsored Bukulo, we've received many letters from him, thanking us for caring and providing for him not only for his physical needs, but also for his education. He's very proud to be the first one in his family to read and he desires to be a doctor one day. Praying for Bukulo became part of our regular prayer time in our family and proved to be just the beginning of a special love and desire to help children that God would put in our hearts. It would be many more years before we'd see the full effect of that passion for children in crisis.

Even as the difficulties and inconveniences of Jarrott's daily care wore on, bright moments of victories and memories stand out to me. His first walk down the block in his wheelchair was exciting. A little ice cream shop was just down the street and we decided to make a family (and nurse) affair of it. Joel pushed Jarrott's wheelchair with the ventilator and oxygen tanks. It weighed over one hundred pounds and was difficult to push. I pulled McKenzie and Brennan in the wagon. The trip down was uneventful, but while we were eating our ice cream, Joel noticed Jarrott's oxygen tanks were almost empty. He had only a few minutes of oxygen left. I'll never forget Joel sprinting down the street, pushing that bulky wheelchair. Jarrott was bouncing up and down and it's a good thing he was strapped in! They made it back with only a moment or two to spare.

His first ride in our van after we got a ramp was a trip to the mall to get pictures. It was scary, yet comical. It took two respiratory therapists, two nurses and an extra babysitter for McKenzie and Brennan. We couldn't even fit in one car. It was exhausting but exhilarating finally being able to do some "normal" activities.

Attending church for the first time together as a family was incredible. For months Joel and I had taken turns attending church while one of us would stay home with Jarrott and the nurse. Occasionally, Melissa would stay with the nurse so Joel and I could go together. But the Sunday finally came when Jarrott and his nurse attended church with us. It was a special day for our church family as well to meet the little boy they'd been lifting up in prayer for so long.

As we at last began to emerge from the long tunnel of suffering, we were starting to get a glimmer of some of the good things God was going to bring about from those interminable months of sorrow.

You Are Good
By Ginger Millermon
© *Anothen Music 2002*

…Well, I have walked
through the valley
I have prayed for hours
On my knees
But You promised
You'd never leave me
And You brought me through faithfully
Lord, you are good to me…

Chapter Thirteen

——

GOD HAS CONTINUED TO take our family on quite an adventure. Two years after the boys were born we were still living in Grand Junction. Life had fallen into a decent routine of scheduling and training nurses, occupational and physical therapy, and frequent doctor appointments for Jarrott. He was in and out of the hospital several times during his first year home, but was slowly stabilizing, his airways and lungs gradually healing.

When the fall of 1998 came around, Joel discovered his position at the nursing home where he assisted in speech therapy was going to be cut by the end of the year. We started praying about what to do. The cost of living in Grand Junction was exorbitant and jobs were scarce. But we were very hesitant to move as we had such good medical care and the doctors there really knew and loved him.

During this time I continued to be under an unreasonable amount of stress. Joel had the opportunity to leave and get away from all of the activity at home when he went to work, but I never really got a break from it. It was day-to-day living with strangers in our home and scheduling our entire life around Jarrott's care and routine. I was exhausted and began to have some health problems, probably directly related to the stress. My mom was driving twelve hours from her home in Kansas every few weeks to assist us and help me get back on my feet so I could take care of our family. It was a cycle of stress that simply wouldn't be broken. My doctor finally sat me down and said something had to change or I would be the one in the hospital next.

After much prayer and seeking counsel, Joel and I decided we should move to Kansas both to be near my family and, importantly, to be in a better economic environment. Jobs were much easier to find and the cost of living much lower in my home state.

Once we decided to make the move, figuring out how to get Jarrott to Kansas became the challenge. He couldn't fly commercially because of his oxygen and equipment. His doctors also strongly advised not trying to drive the seven hundred and fifty miles with him in the car. The altitude over the Continental Divide would be difficult for him and long stretches down the 1-70 corridor had no cell phone service. If Jarrott had a problem enroute, it could be disastrous.

We were starting to have our doubts about our ability to move Jarrott when we heard about an organization called Lifeline that consisted of a group of pilots who would fly people in medical need to doctor appointments or clinics. Once they heard about our dilemma, they were more than willing to fly Jarrott, his nurse, and me to Kansas for free. It was quite a blessing to us and a huge relief to finally have a way to move Jarrott!

Weeks of preparation began as I sought a home health agency with qualified nurses who could care for Jarrott in

Kansas. It was an enormous undertaking, and I was dreading again finding the right nurses to be in our home. We'd grown so close to our nurses and Dr. Pacini; it was very painful to leave and start over. I knew it would also be a big adjustment for Jarrott to accept new nurses. He was starting to want me near him all the time and didn't appreciate all the unfamiliar faces coming into our home to take care of him.

Because he was trached and couldn't talk, we started to do sign language with Jarrott. He picked it up really quickly and his frustration level decreased as he realized he could tell us what he wanted and communicate with us. It was pretty cute as he made up his own signs for McKenzie and Brennan. He asked for them a lot and loved it when they came to play in his room. More than once, all three of the kids and I crawled into his big crib to read books. It was sometimes easier to get into his space than drag all his equipment out to the living room. He really got a kick out of having Mommy in his crib.

The big moving day came in November of 1998. I flew in a little plane with Jarrott and his nurse, Caprice, to Kansas. Caprice was one of the nurses who had really bonded with our family. With short black hair and usually attired in her purple sweat suit, Caprice brought the energy meter in our home to a whole new level. She became a very dear friend, especially competent in the details of Jarrott's care. She spent hours every day talking to him and pushing his heavy wheelchair behind him as he learned to walk. She was concerned, as I was, about how Jarrott would handle the flight with the loud noise of the engine and any turbulence we'd encounter. I was so nervous for him, but had to smile watching Caprice turn green on the bumpy flight. She was terrified of flying, but she was so committed to Jarrott, she volunteered to fly with him. She didn't want anyone else training the new nurses to take care of her "baby." She'd been an incredible nurse to him for many months, and we'd miss her terribly.

As we circled overhead and prepared to land in Hutchinson, I looked down at the runway to see a big group of family and friends waiting with balloons and signs, welcoming Jarrott. I knew it was going to be a good move for our family.

And it was. Within a few days, Jarrott's need for oxygen was gone for the first time in his life. Although he still needed the positive pressure to keep his airways open, he was finally off the oxygen. The lower elevation was really good for him. He continued to progress over the following months and very slowly came off the ventilator, then the C-pap machine, which had provided continuous positive airway pressure. Soon he was independent from all his medical equipment. Getting him decannulated—removing his trach tube—was not so easy.

When he was weaned from all of the equipment, we started to downsize his trach in preparation to remove it permanently. Jarrott was four years old when he went into surgery in Wichita to have the trach removed and his stoma sown shut. We'd told his doctors and nurses that because of his complicated medical history, he was very sensitive about being surrounded by people in masks and gloves. It terrified him, and only Joel or I could keep him calm in that situation. Also, he'd never experienced breathing only from his mouth and nose; all he knew was how to breathe from his trach. We weren't sure how he'd handle that transition. We insisted we needed to be in the recovery room before he woke up to keep him calm, but we were told it was against hospital policy to let parents into the recovery room. We again told his doctors they'd most likely have an emergency on their hands if they refused to let us into recovery.

His surgery went well with no complications. We immediately asked to be taken to the recovery room and reminded the doctor about our concern. He said we'd be called back soon. We sat in the waiting room and waited with growing unease as an hour passed. Finally, our doctor came back out, looking shaken.

"We had some complications in the recovery room. Jarrott woke up and got very upset. We had an emergency situation with him and had to intubate him. He's heavily sedated and on a ventilator."

I could not believe it. After all we'd been through, years of trying to get Jarrott off the ventilator and decannulated, and we were back in the Pediatric Intensive Care Unit with him on a respirator. He had subcutaneous emphysema—air in the tissue under the skin, from his waist to his neck, and a pneumothorax—a hole in his lung. They had to tear out the surgery they had carefully and cosmetically performed to close his stoma to allow him to breathe again through his trach hole. I have to admit it was very difficult for Joel and me to not get angry. We'd done all we could to warn the hospital staff of this possibility and we were ignored. As I have dealt and counseled with families over the years who have children in the hospital, I always remember that frustrating situation and remind parents to be a firm and persistent advocate for their children. No one knows a child like his or her mom or dad. We were definitely "Jarrott" experts. We certainly had some forgiveness issues to work through as we watched Jarrott suffer during that time.

What should have been an outpatient surgery resulted in Jarrott spending nearly a week in the PICU. When it was time to extubate him from the ventilator, his doctors humbly asked us to be in his room right next to his bed. It was a lesson they learned a little too late for us, but hopefully our situation benefited other families who came through that hospital.

After he recovered and came home, it was an incredible day—when for the first time in years, we didn't need any nurses and it was just our family in our home. What a liberating feeling!

And it was a breathtaking moment once his trach was out and I heard his precious laugh for the first time. I'd watched Jarrott's silent giggle for years and to finally hear it made me cry. It was the most beautiful sound I'd ever heard.

Because of all of the medical needs he had, Jarrott was quite delayed in most of his normal development. We continued multiple therapies with him, but were having little success in teaching him to eat by mouth. He was still g-tube fed when he turned four and we were determined to find a way to get him to eat. Because he didn't use his oral muscles to eat, his speech was drastically delayed. In early 2001, after months of research and a yearlong application process, Joel and I drove Jarrott across the country to the Kennedy Krieger Institute in Baltimore, Maryland. Connected with Johns Hopkins University, Kennedy Krieger has a very specialized feeding program to teach orally aversive children how to eat. We were one of only a few families each year accepted into the program. It was a privilege to be part of such an esteemed program, and I knew this was our best chance to teach Jarrott to eat.

It was an exhausting schedule for Jarrott and me over the next two months. At night, I slept in a chair beside his bed in the hospital and he went to hours of therapy every day. I'll never forget one particular day, Jarrott was scheduled to see a neurologist to determine if there was a medical reason he would not eat. They'd run a scan on his brain and the doctor was explaining it to me. He had the scan up on the x-ray viewer and was pointing out problem areas. A social worker attended the appointment with me, a notebook in hand to record comments.

"Well," the neurologist pointed, "here is some damage. This is why your son can't walk and is in a wheelchair..." he continued, but lost me right there. He hadn't met Jarrott yet, and I started to smile. Jarrott had been standing on the other side of me, out of the doctor's view. Within a few seconds, Jarrott came around and stood in front of me, looking up with a grin at the doctor. Surprised, the neurologist looked at Jarrott, then me.

"This isn't Jarrott, right? This is someone else's child." He waited for me to explain.

"No," I smiled, "this is Jarrott." Right then Jarrott started to jump up and down, realizing he had a captive audience.

The doctor's eyes got huge. "This can't be Jarrott!" He pointed excitedly to the scan. "This child can't walk. He can't do that!" He motioned at Jarrott jumping.

"Yes, sir," I assured him, "This is Jarrott."

He was baffled and speechless for a moment as he looked from the scan on the wall to Jarrott. The social worker had been quiet to this point. She finally spoke up and made this profound statement,

"Well, Ginger. This is really a testament to how good of parents you and Joel are."

I laughed. "No," I said firmly, "this was God."

The neurologist looked over at me and nodded his head in affirmation. "This was definitely God. There is no other explanation." He proceeded to ask me if he could take Jarrott's brain scan and show his colleagues at Johns Hopkins. He was completely fascinated by Jarrott. It was an amazing moment to me, knowing Jarrott's story was being told and God was getting the credit. I think I knew then it was only the beginning of our telling an amazing story about our amazing God.

Jarrott and I were in Baltimore for nearly ten weeks that spring and it was tough...but it was also worth it. I missed Brennan and McKenzie and Joel terribly, but by the time we came home, Jarrott was getting enough calories by mouth that we were able to remove his g-tube. And he finally started to talk. And once he started to talk, there was no stopping him!

Several years have gone by quickly and quite eventfully. But I have to tell you, the little baby who was going to have "no quality of life," as I write this book, is a healthy eleven-year-old boy. He has had several eye surgeries over the years and has some on-going struggles with his vision and learning challenges. But the medical world continues to be fascinated by him, more than once calling him a "modern day miracle." He loves to ride his bike, wrestle with Brennan, tease McKenzie, and play baseball. Not long ago, at a radio interview with Focus on the Family, Jarrott declared he wanted to be a pastor someday. Because, as he states in his own words, "I just want to preach and stuff." I bet he'll have a lot to say.

The journey in our family is by no means over. Our friends shake their heads at the continuing Millermon saga and wonder what kind of chemistry must have collided in the universe when Joel and I married. Consider for instance the time we thought we might lose Brennan to high altitude pulmonary edema while up in the mountains; or the year McKenzie spent in a wheelchair and on crutches from double foot surgery because of a genetic bone problem; or perhaps the time Brennan and Joel were chased by a bear on a hunting trip. All that to say, you'd think by now we would have had enough drama and excitement to last a lifetime.

But we did find another adventure we simply had to embark on. And this quest would take us around the globe.

I mentioned previously that God has given us a heart for children in crisis. Joel and I work in our concert and conference ministry to bring hope to children, and have been privileged to travel to both the Dominican Republic and Uganda to see the impact child sponsorship has in those poverty stricken areas. God took that passion for children in crisis, and allowed it to blossom into something far more tangible than I could have ever planned. We're currently in the process of adopting a beautiful little girl from India. She's an abandoned three-year-old orphan who needs our family desperately, and we're thrilled to give her a home and a family. We're planning to travel to India to bring her home soon. I'm guessing that adventure might be a whole new story.

It has been quite a journey. Filled with anguish and despair on one hand, but swelling victory and deepening faith on the other. Filling these pages and reliving some of the darkest days of my life has brought me to my knees several times both in sorrow and extreme gratefulness. I'm increasingly thankful God allowed our family to endure through the fire. He has tested us, molded us, changed us and irrevocably impressed His holiness, sovereignty and mercy on our hearts and minds.

I'm so glad on that long ago Tuesday—August 6, 1996—my life changed forever. To God be the glory!

We are Amazed
By Paul Marino and Ginger Millermon
2007 Van Ness Press, Inc. (ASCAP)/McKinney
Music, Inc. (BMI) (both admin. by LifeWay Worship Music Group).

Lord, we are amazed
At the splendor or Your ways
Nothing can compare
To Your glory
Lord, we lift our hearts
And with our voices raised
We sing a song of praise to You
We are amazed
We love You, Jesus
We are amazed
Lord, we are amazed
At the beauty of Your grace
And nothing can compare
To Your mercy
Lord, we stand in awe
At the wonder of it all
We sing a song of praise to You

Our first official
family photo, August 1997.
Jarrott was still in the hospital
but almost ready to come home.

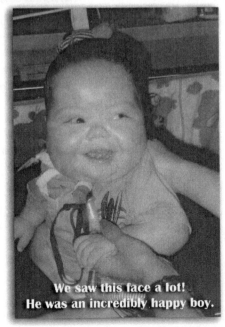

We saw this face a lot!
He was an incredibly happy boy.

Not long after Jarrott came home from the hospital. They became great buddies!

Best friends riding scooters!

Kindergarten graduation.

Catching his first
fish with Daddy.

A Note From Dr. Ann Olewnik:

I first met Jarrott about eleven years ago at St. Mary's Hospital in Grand Junction, Colorado when he made his arrival into this world ten weeks early and needed to be in a neonatal intensive care unit. I was one of many doctors and health professionals who would be involved with Jarrott's care for many years. I don't think I can completely or accurately convey just how sick Jarrott was in these few lines of text, but suffice it to say he was one the sickest premature babies I have ever cared for who has survived. Some of the most challenging yet gratifying moments of my professional life occurred while I cared for Jarrott. I will never forget him or his wonderful family.

At first, Jarrott seemed like he'd follow a typical and relatively uneventful medical course in dealing with his premature lungs and respiratory distress syndrome; however he quickly and unfortunately demonstrated that his lungs were much more fragile than his twin brother Brennan's. Jarrott went on to develop what we now call chronic lung disease of prematurity and his chronic lung disease was especially devastating. In chronic lung disease of prematurity, the baby's lung becomes inflamed and swollen with fluid. The structure and normal growth of the lung tissue are disrupted, and scar tissue replaces normal lung tissue. Although this condition can occur in premature babies who have never been on a ventilator, it is usually worse in those infants who require ventilator support to treat their respiratory distress syndrome. As we watched Brennan improve and eventually come off ventilator support, Jarrott became more ill...more dependent on the ventilator to keep him alive. With premature lungs, one of the cruel realities is that although the ventilator is keeping the premature baby alive, it inevitably causes damage to the delicate, underdeveloped tissue of the lung. This is why doctors make every effort to minimize the time a baby stays on a ventilator. So, in Jarrott's case, the longer he needed to stay on the ventilator, the more damage his lungs sustained. The more damage his lungs sustained, the more difficult it became to wean him off the ventilator.

After failing to get Jarrott off the conventional type of ventilator that was commonly in use at the time he was born, we made a decision to send him to The Children's Hospital in Denver where there were more options for treatment. Although I was not providing medical care for Jarrott while he was in Denver, I kept in phone contact with his doctors and with Ginger and Joel. Jarrott did not respond well to the rescue therapies, which were used in the hopes of quickly weaning him off ventilator support. Instead, he developed severe chronic lung disease and eventually got to a point where his doctors in Denver were convinced he would die. There seemed to be nothing left to offer Jarrott. He was on maximal life support with the newest and best treatments that neonatology and pediatric pulmonology had to offer. I remember talking to Ginger by phone just before Christmas in 1996, and she was telling me how she, Joel and their family were trying to prepare themselves for Jarrott's death.

And then, Jarrott started to get better and it looked like he might survive. This was the beginning of a long road of what seemed like miraculous ups and terrifying downs for Jarrott and his family. Although Jarrott came back to St. Mary's Hospital eventually for convalescent care in preparation for going home, he was still a critically ill baby. He needed a tracheotomy for a more permanent breathing tube in his airway so he could go home on a ventilator. He needed a feeding tube placed directly into his stomach through the abdominal wall because he could not eat normally. He had visual problems. He had neurological deficits. Because of the severity of his lung disease and the complications of being on a ventilator for such a prolonged period of time, Jarrott had numerous episodes where his oxygen levels in the blood were so low and his carbon dioxide levels in his blood were so toxic that all of his doctors were certain he'd have severe brain damage. My partners and I were convinced on more than one occasion that Jarrott would never leave the hospital alive.

When I look back over that time, I remember thinking that in spite of all the medical science and clinical expertise we utilized to care for Jarrott and try to predict his outcome, someone else was really calling the shots. Just as I was certain that Jarrott was going to die, he'd start to recover and improve. One of my physician partners had an expression he used when Jarrott seemed to pull himself back from death's doorstep (which he did on numerous occasions). He would usually say this after Jarrott required vigorous resuscitation measures to help him recover from one of his many abrupt pulmonary deteriorations. After we all would look at each other in awe of the fact that this little boy survived another major setback, my partner would say, "Well, Jarrott just made a fool out of all of us again!" I like to think this was really the hand of God giving us a little tap on the shoulder to let us know that Jarrott wasn't ready to give up yet.

Even after Jarrott went home, he and his family had what seemed like insurmountable hurdles to deal with. Again, based on medical science and statistical odds, I was not convinced that he could survive at home. He had many life-threatening emergencies at home and many re-hospitalizations for serious setbacks.

But…Jarrott is here today and is doing better than any of us could have ever dreamed. Even though he had the most sophisticated medical care available at the time, I think it was hope, faith and determination that really pulled Jarrott through this ordeal.

Jarrott has already done so much for me personally and professionally as a result of his presence. I think God still has more for Jarrott to teach us all about caring for each other with love and compassion, having faith and strength of character, and being courageous in the face of overwhelming adversity. I'm honored to have been part of Jarrott's and his family's lives. I thank them all for the priceless lessons they have taught me. Jarrott, you continue to delight and amaze me! I can't wait to hear about the next chapter in your life!

———

Ann B. Olewnik, MD, Fellow of the American Academy of Pediatrics
Former Medical Director, Division of Neonatology
St. Mary's Hospital and Medical Center
Grand Junction, Colorado

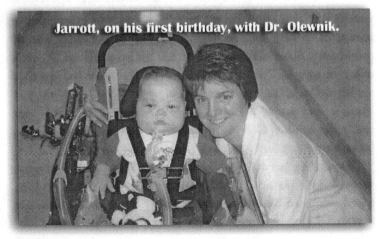

Jarrott, on his first birthday, with Dr. Olewnik.

Epilogue

Our Adoption Journey

I HAVE TO REITERATE HOW grateful I am that God doesn't let us
see the whole picture all at once. Had I known what this new
exploit would involve, I wonder if I would have been brave
enough to see it through.

But let me back up for just a minute, because looking
back, I can see so many ways that God was getting us ready
for a new chapter in our lives. The summer of 2006 was a
busy one for us. We had toured the East Coast for 10 weeks
on the weekends with the whole family and during the
weekdays had been on staff at Word of Life Inn and
Conference Center in New York. We helped with the 150
teens on staff and I was a guest artist in residence for the
summer. We came home exhausted yet fulfilled after being
able to serve and minister all summer. When Word of Life
asked us to return the next summer, we readily agreed. Joel's
experience as a youth pastor made it an easy transition for us
and although being gone from home for so many weeks had its
difficulties, we loved it. We booked our summer of 2007

weekends with concerts and women's conferences all over the East Coast and made our plans to tour again. So, I can't tell you how dismayed I was when the director at Word of Life called us one afternoon in late March with some disappointing news.

He got right to the point, "Ginger, our needs here have changed and we aren't going to be able to use you and Joel with the teens this summer."

I felt a spiral of alarm. What on earth were we going to do? We already had our weekends booked and would have nowhere to be during the week if we weren't at Word of Life. We would have to cancel our tour.

But he wasn't finished. "Although we can't use you with the teens, I'd really like you and Joel to head up our kids program for the summer. You'd be in charge of the daycare and the programming for all of the guests' kids that come each week. Ages zero to twelve."

Okay, that's when full-blown panic set in! Running a daycare? Being responsible for hundreds of small children for the summer? I mean, yeah, I'm a mom and I like my kids and all and I've sort of gotten them figured out...but being in charge of other peoples' children terrified me—especially the little ones. It had been a long time since my own were that young. Word of Life had a reputation for having a wonderful program for the children while the parents were in Bible meetings. The kids program was key to making those weeks successful.

Joel and I look back and laugh now because he says I had a "psycho look" in my eyes for weeks. I prayed for the rapture like never before. Surely Jesus could come back before the summer started.

Well, He didn't come back and I went into that venture full of trepidation. My main prayer was not that the children would learn or have a wonderful time; I simply wanted them all to survive the summer. High expectations indeed.

Well, the point in this little vignette is this: over those weeks, the panic slowly faded and I remembered how much fun little kids are. I pushed babies in strollers, changed diapers, held screaming, mad toddlers and chased down the ones who tried to escape. By the end of the summer, my staff of thirteen teenage girls ran like a well-oiled machine and I had conquered my apprehension of small children. I had adapted and learned to be flexible and grew so much that summer. And God, like always, knew *exactly* what He was doing to prepare me for the next big thing.

When we returned home after the long summer on the road, we didn't have much time to recuperate. We had a busy fall schedule ahead as well as getting the kids back into school. Shortly after we arrived home I noticed we had received an email from friends who had adopted from Russia. Occasionally, they would forward emails from their adoption agency of children who desperately needed homes. To be honest, I almost always deleted the emails without opening them. I knew seeing the pictures of the children would tear me up and I didn't think adopting was an option for us—at least not at this point in life. In previous years, Joel and I had talked about adopting, more in passing conversation. It was something we might consider when the kids were almost grown—not while they were still young and we were traveling full time. I love how God just blasts me out of my comfort zone sometimes.

I don't know why I opened that particular email from my friend that day. It just said something about gorgeous little girls in India who needed homes. The instant I opened the email, ten beautiful brown faces filled the screen. My eyes landed on a little face that literally took my breath away: a three-year-old little girl named Shasmita with snappy dark eyes and choppy black hair. My heart started to pound and I clicked the email closed. But there was something about her that kept drawing me back. I found myself getting up at night and opening the email. I would zoom up on her face and study every feature. I couldn't get her out of my mind. Finally, after a couple of days of secretly looking at her picture, I casually mentioned it to Joel.

"Did you open that email about the little girls from India?"

"Yeah, I saw them," he replied.

"So...did any of them stand out to you?" I clicked open the email.

"Actually, two of them did. I thought they kind of looked like Kenzie when she was little." He reached across my desk and pointed at Shasmita and another little girl.

"Yeah, me too! That little one named Shasmita keeps jumping out at me. I think about her constantly. What do you think that means?" I asked.

Before he could answer, McKenzie walked into our office. "Hey, Kenz, look at these little girls from India. Aren't they cute?" I didn't mention these were girls up for adoption.

McKenzie instantly pointed to Shasmita. "That's the one, Mom."

That's the one? I looked up at Joel, both of us stunned. I think we knew at that point that we needed to take a serious look at what God was trying to tell us. Over the next several days we researched, called the adoption agency and prayed hard. There was no question that we were willing to bring a child into our home. But we didn't have a normal life. We were on the road nearly every weekend, sometimes for weeks at a time. Our children had adapted but how would a new addition from another culture change the dynamics of our family and ministry? I knew from other people's stories that

there were often very rough times with bonding and
behavioral issues bringing a child from an orphanage situation.
Frankly, it scared me to death! We had friends question our
sanity and ask if we were going to give up the ministry. I
didn't know all the answers but as God quickly removed one
obstacle after another, it became clear to Joel and I that this
was an obedience issue. God had put this precious child on
our hearts and had paved the way for us to adopt her. Even
the financial expense, which seemed insurmountable, had
been provided by God in a miraculous way. We were either
going to step out in faith and obey, or tell God no. Telling
God "no" scared us a whole lot more than adopting so we
jumped in with both feet. And God time and again amazed us
with His provision and attention to the very last detail. Soon
there was no doubt in our minds—we were going to India!

One year later in August of 2008, paperwork done and
documents in hand, we boarded a plane to travel around the
world to bring our daughter home. We had no idea the
excitement that would be waiting for us in India.

I had been told by several people who had traveled to India
that you'll know you are there by the variety of smells that
assault you when you step off the plane. For me it wasn't the
smell as much as the suffocating humidity. It stole the breath
right out of me. Of course, we hit Delhi in the middle of
monsoon season so we were met with both scorching heat and
extreme humidity.

Our contact in India, through our adoption agency, was a
gentleman by the name of Rajeev. Over the course of the
week we spent there, I came to respect this man so much. He
had been a successful businessman selling women's high
fashion shoes. (I knew there was a reason I liked him!) Yet he
became so burdened for the children suffering in his country,
he gave up his business and dedicated his life to helping

orphans. He was our liaison in the court system, our interpreter and guide, and by the end of the week, our dear friend. He had worked non-stop over the past year to get our papers through the court system as quickly as possible—which is no small job.

We arrived in India the evening of August 23rd and Rajeev met us at the airport. I'll never forget being so nervous walking out of the airport and seeing the hundreds of people waiting and holding signs. I wondered how we would ever find Rajeev.

Suddenly, I heard a voice calling, "Ginga! Ginga!" I looked over and there was a short, middle-aged Indian man with a big smile waving us down. He ushered us to his vehicle and took us to our hotel for the night. We still had to fly to the state of Orissa in northeast India the next day. We were to meet up with Rajeev and another couple, Mike and Jill Turner, who were also adopting their daughter, Sova, from Shasmita's orphanage. It was such a blessing to meet Mike and Jill the next morning. We quickly realized that they were a fantastic Christian couple and we had much in common. God knew that we would need each other's support throughout the trauma the next 48 hours would bring.

We had an afternoon flight so Rajeev took us out for a bit of sightseeing. He suggested his favorite coffee shop and I wasn't about to argue with that! I journaled a few details of our first day in Delhi:

Delhi is very different in the daylight. Our cars were constantly bombarded with children selling American magazines in the streets. Every time our cars would stop in traffic there would be taps on our windows and begging brown eyes. It was so hard to shake our heads and turn away. An old woman stood begging at our car rubbing her empty belly. Made us incredibly sad. It was such a helpless feeling. The children standing in the road were the hardest. We saw one little boy, maybe 10-12 years old, walking down the median with no clothes on at all. Not a stitch.

It was emotional upheaval for me just driving through Delhi. We also stopped briefly in the market to pick up a few things for the girls. Shopping in Delhi was an experience. We certainly had to watch our step as there were cows everywhere! We just had to walk around them to get to the shops. They would sometimes have garlands of flowers around their heads—a reminder that cows are revered and protected in the Hindu religion. Seeing the incredible amount of people wandering the streets, the begging children, sometimes blind or without limbs, made the senselessness of honoring cows particularly hard for me. Children starving while animals are honored. India is truly a lost country in desperate need of the Gospel of Jesus Christ.

After shopping, we headed to the airport to catch our flight to Orissa. Just before boarding the flight, Mike turned to me.

"I forgot to tell you...did you hear about the bombings in Orissa this morning?" He asked. That's not really the kind of thing you want to hear as you're boarding the plane.

"No..." I said slowly. "What's going on?"

He said he wasn't sure but there was some violence erupting in Orissa. There had been bombings or perhaps an assassination. I wondered what would meet us when we landed.

The flight seemed endless as hundreds of miles of India passed beneath us and it was dark when we arrived in Bhubaneswar, the capital city in Orissa. There was a tension that we noticed immediately, even at the airport. People's glances weren't nearly as friendly as in Delhi. Two drivers met us outside and we got into the car with Rajeev and his driver. He immediately began speaking in Hindi, asking rapid questions. Joel and I were silent in the back seat, hoping to pick up any information. Rajeev got on his cell phone and began making calls. I didn't understand much but I did hear the words "strike tomorrow."

Our drivers dropped us at the hotel and as we checked in, the hotel manager wanted us to leave our passports at the desk with him. We were all adamant that we wanted our passports back so we watched as they made copies of each of our passports and filed them away, giving us back our originals. Before we went to our rooms for the night, Rajeev explained the situation the best that he knew at that point.

Apparently, the president of a radical Hindu group had been assassinated. Hindu extremists had taken to the streets hunting down and persecuting Christians. We wouldn't know the horror of the full situation for some time. What Rajeev knew for sure is that there would be a strike the next day. No shops would be open, no cars allowed on the streets. Shops that opened would be torched; people who took their cars out were at risk of being shot. Rajeev was not sure what we were going to do and suggested he might even rent an ambulance to sneak us to the orphanage or perhaps we would go at night under cover of darkness. After much discussion, he suggested we get some sleep and he would contact us in the morning. He was staying at a hotel down the street and before he left he advised us not to leave the hotel for any reason. When we asked why, he said that because we were American, people would assume we were Christian. If we were to go outside, we might be harmed.

We were a somber bunch as we headed to our rooms. We noticed right away that there appeared to be no other guests in the hotel. Two Indian men led us down several back hallways to our rooms. It was one of the creepiest things I've ever experienced! I felt like I was in the middle of an Alfred

Hitchcock movie. We made sure we had Mike and Jill's hotel room phone number and gave them ours. We promised to call if we needed anything.

As soon as we were in our room, we grabbed our computer and started sending emails to our parents and a few close friends, asking for prayer:

We have a challenge ahead for us. There have been bombings in Orissa today. It's been all over the news. Rajeev is not sure how tomorrow will go. There is a big strike and getting to and from the orphanage is uncertain. Rajeev hasn't told us the whole plan but I did hear him say something about possibly getting them at night or renting an ambulance for tomorrow so we can get to the orphanage and back. Just pray that if we are supposed to do this that he would be able to get it and if not that this would fall through. Rajeev has assured us several times if he feels it is not safe for us to go tomorrow in the ambulance, we will not go. He is very careful so we trust him to make the right decision. You knew it would be an extra ordinary adventure for the Millermons to be in India. I feel sorry for the couple we are traveling with. They did not sign up for travel with us! Please give the kids our love but don't mention this to them. They do not need to be worrying. When it's all over we'll tell them. It is good to remember at this point that God is the One ultimately in control. None of these circumstances take Him by surprise at all. We are right where we are supposed to be, getting our precious girl, so there is no safer place in the world for us right now.

It was a fitful night's sleep for us and we were up very early preparing for the day. We wondered nervously if we would soon be hunkering down in the back of an ambulance sneaking to the orphanage. We hoped to have good news from Rajeev—perhaps that the violence had stopped and we could proceed with our original plans. But as we turned the television on that morning in our room, we saw more and more footage of the carnage that was taking place. Churches were on fire; cars and tires were burning in the streets. We would find out later that this day in Orissa was the worst religious persecution documented in Asia for decades. Literally hundreds of Christians were martyred that day and thousands fled to the forests for protection. Dozens of churches were burned; pastors were sought out, tortured and murdered. As we watched the news in stunned disbelief, we were horrified to hear that an orphanage had been burned down and children were missing. We didn't have any reference for where things were in Orissa. We knew we were still a distance from the orphanage but we didn't know if the violence was close to Cuttack where the orphanage was located.

Rajeev finally called late in the morning and we rushed to meet him and the Turners in the lobby.

He let us know quickly of his decision. "We will not be able to go today. I did not hire the ambulance. It is not safe. You must stay inside."

I was relieved and disappointed at the same time. Relieved that we weren't taking the risk, but crushed that there was no way we were getting our little girl that day. We had waited more than a year for this day to come.

Rajeev instructed us to wait at the hotel while he continued to monitor the situation and make new plans. We walked slowly back to our rooms and wondered quietly if the hotel was safe for us. The men working at the hotel constantly were talking right outside our rooms. We could see them in the halls on their cell phones and we had to wonder if they were telling friends about the two American couples staying at the hotel. They knew what rooms we were in and had copies of our passports. We felt very vulnerable. We decided that it would be better for all of us if we were in the same room. We invited Mike and Jill to come to our room to pray through the day. We continued to send email updates to family. I sent one particular email to my two closest friends:

> *Kris and Staci,*
>
> *I am emailing just you two because I want to be bluntly honest but not pass this information on just yet. We really don't want to worry our parents and kids but if something were to happen, please let them know this information.*
>
> *Sounds quite morbid I know, but we don't feel our situation here is safe. We are holed up at the hotel, not to go outside and let people see us. The Hindus are burning churches, there was an assassination here yesterday of a prominent leader and the Hindus are blaming the Christians. Rajeev is telling us to stay in the hotel. Jill and Mike are across the hall from us. They came to our room and we are staying and praying together. Their room opens into a closed courtyard while ours opens into a garden so we feel like if we had to make an escape, our room is better. I can't believe we have to think about this but that's where we are. We really need wisdom on how to proceed. Rajeev says the strike will end mid-day although we wonder in a situation this volatile how it will suddenly be safe for us to travel on the roads. He is talking about us going closer to dark to the orphanage, getting the girls quickly and coming back to the hotel. Sort of a covert mission. You know I love adventure but this is getting ridiculous! Very much just feeling like we want to get our girl and get back to Delhi and home to our kids.*

It's hard to explain, but that day ended up being a precious one. We spent lots of time praying and came to such a peace of knowing God was fully in control. I wish we had known the full extent of what was happening outside of the city. We would have spent more time in fervent prayer for our brothers and sisters in Christ who were dying that very day for their faith.

By mid-afternoon Rajeev came back for us and we decided to switch hotels to be closer to him. He thought it was safe enough for us to walk down the street. It was eerily quiet outside as we dragged our suitcases behind us to the Ginger Hotel. (What a great name for a hotel!) Cars were still prohibited on the streets so the usual incessant honking was silent. As we were crossing the street, a motorcyclist pointed and screamed at us all the way down the road. We felt exposed and uncomfortable being outside. After we got settled, Rajeev had to find a way to get to the airport and change our plane tickets. We were to have flown back to Delhi that afternoon and needed new tickets. Much to our dismay, Rajeev hired a motorcyclist to take him to the airport. He had to have our passports to change our tickets and I can't begin to express how nervous we were when he took off with a perfect stranger, our passports in his pocket! But he returned safely an hour later, our tickets changed for the next evening. He told us he laughed all the way to the airport because of the looks on our faces when he left. His confidence was never shaken and his competence was a tremendous comfort to us. He assured us that the strike and riots would be over by six o'clock and we would go to the orphanage in the morning. That was totally confusing to me! How could a strike end on schedule? I tried to explain to Rajeev that in America, a strike or riot ends when someone *makes* it end. He patiently told me just to wait and see. And he was right! As the afternoon slipped into evening, cars started honking and congesting the streets again. Things seemed to be progressing back to normal, at least in Bhubaneswar. We were feeling relieved and hopeful as we sat down to dinner in our hotel that night. But in the middle of laughing and eating, the electricity suddenly went out. Rajeev seemed uncon-cerned and kept eating but the Turners and Joel and I exchanged nervous glances. We wondered if the violence was starting up again. As I mentioned, the people, particularly the men in Orissa, were not nearly as open and friendly as in Delhi. The café was full of Indian men openly watching us, and the electricity surging off and on did not help our apprehension. We were once again very grateful for Rajeev's calm presence.

Late in the day, Rajeev invited Joel and I to his room to use his computer to email an update to our family. As I was typing emails, Joel and Rajeev were sitting on his bed talking. It suddenly occurred to me that this would be the perfect opportunity to share Christ with Rajeev. We had been praying that we would have a chance sometime that week. Especially in Orissa with the persecution happening, we didn't feel like we could openly talk in the café or airport. This might be our only chance for privacy.

Joel was on the same page and was praying for the right way to start the conversation when Rajeev spoke up.

"I am so sick of religion," he stated emphatically. Joel and I were both stunned! We hadn't even been talking about spiritual things. That opened the door perfectly for Joel to share the gospel with Rajeev over the next hour. I think it was one of the most beautiful moments of my life when the three of us knelt beside his bed and Rajeev prayed to ask Jesus to be his Savior. I'll never forget the look in his eyes when he finished praying.

He smiled at us and said, "That is quite a feeling!" The peace and joy on his face was evident. We had brought a new believer's Bible and some other books on the trip that we were able to pass along to him. It really hit me that night as we got ready to go to sleep—God is so amazing. Just when I was wondering why the riots had to happen the day we flew in, changing our whole schedule, scaring us and adding turmoil to the trip, God had plans beyond my imagination. We weren't just sent to India to rescue an abandoned orphan, we were sent to India to share Christ's love with Rajeev. And as one little girl's physical life was being changed by adoption, one man's spiritual life was rescued from eternal separation from God.

We went to bed that night praising God for Rajeev's salvation and praying fervently that things would be settled down and safe by morning. Once again, I had to go back to God's promises that He would never leave us, never forsake us, and that He had good plans for our lives.

Although there continued to be violence in outlying areas the next morning, things were much better in our region. The Turners had prayed the night before that God would send rain in the morning to keep people off the streets and away from our cars as we traveled. Boy, did their prayer get answered! We awoke to monsoon winds and rains, bending the trees nearly to the ground.

We made our way safely to the orphanage and the rain tapered off and stopped as we reached the gates to go in. As we pulled through the gate between high, cement walls, we could see children excitedly running through the front garden. The orphanage was a large, three story cement structure, painted a pale yellow. There were covered terraces on the outside of each floor and the children were racing back and forth pointing at our cars and clapping.

As I got out of our car, I saw a tiny girl run by in a red dress yelling, "Mommy, Daddy! Mommy, Daddy!" I knew that was my first glimpse of our daughter. But a nanny whisked her away before I could get a good look at her. They had a very specific order in which things were done when parents arrived for their children. I was almost overcome by emotion at this point. I wanted to just skip their order and grab my girl! I couldn't wait to finally hold her.

We were taken first to meet the director of the orphanage. We had brought donations with us and she was very grateful, especially for the bags of toothbrushes for the children. After the introductions, we were led to a room on the third floor and noticed a wooden sign above the door that said, "Meet Your Child." This was the room! We asked that Shasmita and Sova be brought one at a time so that we could video-tape for the Turners and they could in turn video our first moments with Shas.

About twenty minutes passed and we finally heard someone call, "Here is Sova!" We quickly prepared the cameras and watched in tears as Sova was introduced to Mike and Jill. She was all dressed up and very shy as she approached her new parents.

Before we knew it, Rajeev called out, "Here comes Shasmita!" We scrambled to switch cameras and Mike started filming as she walked in the room. She was the cutest thing in the world. She was dressed in a blue floral shirt with matching white and blue capri pants. Her hair was buzzed short and she had little sparkly sticker earrings on and a dot on her forehead. She was smiling but hesitant as we knelt and held out our arms to her. She seemed like she was in a daze and her nanny finally gave her a little shove toward us. She just stood there, grinning at us, and Joel moved forward first and she finally put her arms around him. Joel held her tight and said, "Daddy" to which she sweetly responded, "Daddy." It was now my turn. I gave her a hug and said, "Mommy!" while pointing to myself. She quickly repeated "Mommy" after me, smiling hugely. She was obviously excited to meet us yet overwhelmed just like we were. It was so cute as she echoed back everything we said. We said, "I love you," over and over and she would say it too, not having a clue what she was saying. We spent a long time in the room hugging and talking and playing. We brought a little stuffed pink bear for her and she loved it.

After a good length of time in our "meeting" room, we moved down to a play room with the other children. Sova and Shas played with their friends and we interacted with the other children. They were all so hungry to be loved, holding up their arms to us, crawling on our laps. When we left the playroom we had a tour of the nursery. There were several dozen children ranging from newborns to three-year-olds in this large room. Many of the children and babies were lying or playing on the cement floor. While it was nothing like we would imagine an American orphanage to be, I was pleased to see how many blocks, riding toys and other fun things were available for the children, as well as the loving interaction and care shown to them by their nannies. Some of the older kids were holding the smaller ones. I noticed several children with special needs and one little boy in particular really tugged at my heart. He was blind and was sitting alone at the side of the room. I walked over to him and talked to him quietly. When I put my hands on the sides of his face, he leaned into my hands and smiled. I sat on the floor with him for quite some time praying over him and touching his face. He seemed so content just to feel my hands on his face. As I looked over the room, there were many children just sitting on the floor alone, some playing, others crying. As attentive as the nannies were, there were so many children that required attention. There was no way the nannies were able to fill each child's emotional and physical needs. They needed homes and families. I knew when we prepared to go to the orphanage that it would be difficult to see the other children and not be able to take them as well. It was beyond difficult; it was unspeakably painful to leave the other children behind.

One of the highlights of my day was visiting with several older girls who were still waiting to go home to their families. They were practicing their English on me and while Shas took a nap next to me, these beautiful girls sang, danced and told me all about their families in America. They even ran to their rooms to get the photo albums their families had sent. They proudly showed me all their relatives they would have when they finally got home. I found out which areas of the country the girls were going to and told them as much as I could about their particular state. It was a precious time of encouraging them and listening to their stories.

As we prepared to leave later in the afternoon, there was a ceremony that had to be done first. It was tradition for the nannies to paint the girls and ladies feet and nails red. We sat in Shas' room while her nanny painted my all my nails and then dyed my feet red with a dark stain, painting flowers and designs on top of my feet. Then she repeated the ceremony on Shas. I remember thinking as the dye seeped into my toenails, "This is never going to come off and all I brought to wear are flip-flops!" It was quite a sight!

Finally, one of the nannies brought shoes for Shas and Sova to put on. It was a sign to all of the children that we were leaving. None of the kids wore shoes except as they left the orphanage with their families. Some of the nannies started to weep and Shas and Sova's closest friends cried loudly as we loaded up in the cars. The girls both started in as well, and as we pulled through the gates to catch our flight back to Delhi, I prayed that the children who remained would very soon be going home to families of their own.

Shas was pretty emotional starting out our first flight. It was late and we were both relieved when she finally fell asleep. We didn't arrive back at our hotel in Delhi until nearly midnight. That's when Joel and I realized we had quite a job ahead of us before we would get any sleep. Our hotel room had one big, king-sized bed that we all would share. That was fine—except Shas, to our knowledge, had never had a bath and her short, black hair was covered with lice. We broke out the lice medication and combs and each took a side of her head. It was a long, tedious job and by the time she was all combed out, she still needed to have her bath and medication applied to her hair. She had no idea what to do in a bathtub full of water. I'm pretty sure they heard her screaming clear in the lobby! She was scared, exhausted and totally done with us by the time that was over! After long stretches of crying, she finally fell asleep. Thankfully, she woke up in the morning no worse for the wear. I sent an email that morning:

Oh my goodness she's so cute this morning! She slept really well. Woke up once in the night and looked at Joel and went back to sleep. We only got a couple hours sleep but who cares! We have Shas! She is so sweet in her new yellow jammies. We asked her if she needed to potty (Ku-jee-boh) and she nodded and did great. Yesterday, at the orphanage she and Sova both just pulled their pants down and went in the middle of the floor. We were all thinking, "Wow! That's going to go over great in the airport!" So far communication has been just fine. She is super smiley this morning, looking out the window and jabbering away. She thinks her daddy is hilarious. He's making faces and talking and being silly and she is loving it.

I can't even imagine what is going through her mind this morning after leaving the conditions of the orphanage and being in this hotel filled with luxury. Wow. Her life has changed.

For Kenzi, Jar, Bren and G'ma and Papa: Be prepared for the

*most skilled cold shoulder you've ever seen! She is a pro. She will stare
you down and make you feel an inch high if she's not in the mood for
you. She is totally cracking us up.*

She picked up communication so quickly. We had brought
a book of pictures of basic objects so we could start to teach
her some words. Joel had given her an apple that was in our
hotel room the first morning. The next morning, she got up,
picked up her new book, flipped to the page showing an apple
and pointed expectantly. She wanted another apple. We were
amazed. She was also *very* excited about all the new clothes
and shoes. She had never had anything of her own so she was
understandably in awe of the new wardrobe. When I got her
dressed that first morning complete with new shoes and a
pink headband, we could barely pull her away from the
mirror.

The rest of our week in India flew by in a flurry of
necessary activities. We had several trips to the embassy to
make; medical releases and paperwork to fill out; and a little
bit of shopping for some treasures to give to Shas when she is
older. We had also planned to visit the Taj Mahal if there was
time and since our embassy work went quickly, we got
started on the four-hour trip to Agra. That is one car ride I
will never forget!

*We were going right through rush hour getting out of Delhi. I
don't care where you live in the U.S.; it is nothing like rush hour in
Delhi! You are not only fighting traffic, but also cows, dogs, donkeys,
goats, bicycles, and anything else you can imagine! People will just
walk in the streets and expect you to not run over them. I haven't seen
one wreck but driving here is terrifying! Buses will be coming at you
head on and you think "this is it!" and at the very last second
someone swerves. With the crazy driving, I started to get very sick and
about half way to Agra I had to get out. I went behind this really
gross gas station and threw up. I'm standing there vomiting and*

*monkeys are screaming in the trees above me, cars are honking, and I
was getting eaten alive by mosquitoes probably carrying malaria. I
thought, "What on earth am I doing in the middle of India?"
Actually, I can sort of laugh about it now but I was thinking at the
time "I'm not going to make it!"*

Rajeev was so sweet on that long car ride. He knew how
miserable I was and when I got back into the car, he turned
around and handed me his cell phone.

"Call your parents," he said with a smile. I think I must
have looked like death. I hadn't been able to call home and it
was such a blessing to check in with the kids and hear their
voices.

Agra is Rajeev's hometown and he graciously invited us to
his home to meet his wife and share a meal. We spent the
night at a little hotel and in the morning we all took the girls
out for their first swim in a pool. It was a little chilly in the
early morning so they weren't real impressed. Later in the
day we went to the Taj Mahal. What an incredible, beautiful
place. I'd like to say I appreciated it as much as it deserved,
but to be honest, it was very stressful. It was extremely hot
and humid that day; I have never been so hot in my life. But
the worst part was, Shas had decided that she didn't like me,
she only wanted daddy. If I would try to hold her or take her
hand, she would scream and fall to the ground. We were
aware going into the adoption that often a child bonds with
one adoptive parent before the other. Now, I knew this but I
thought *surely* she would bond with me! After all, I am a
mommy! But it was her daddy she wanted and when I would
try to get near her, she would cry and throw fits. We were all
pretty emotional on the trip back to Delhi.

The trip to get home was extremely long and difficult.
While she slept on most of the flight from Delhi to London,
there were a lot of tears for Shas and I on the flight from

London to Chicago, both of us exhausted and frustrated.

We finally reached the Wichita airport. Shas was barely staying awake but managed to give Kenzi, Brennan and Jarrott a few smiles and hugs. They were thrilled with their new, little sister. They loved listening to her words and songs in Oryian, her native language. She came home knowing just a few English words. While she could recite some of the alphabet and months of the year, she had no idea what they meant. She *did* know and understand the words 'mommy,' 'daddy' and 'cookie.' And when you're four-years old, what else do you really need to know?

The first few weeks were pretty tough, especially for me. Shas would cry herself to sleep, not letting us comfort her. She went through a grieving process as she missed her nanny and friends. She watched me from a distance and tolerated me giving her all the "good" stuff. I made sure I was the one giving her toys, yummy food and her baths that she eventually loved. Even with all of that, she did not want me to touch her or hold her for quite some time. But as she watched the other kids love on mommy, she started to decide that I was probably okay. It seemed like forever, but it was only a few weeks before she was hugging me and giving me good night kisses.

At some point during that time, I was struck by a sobering thought: I had sacrificed and prayed for this child for more than a year. I had planned, cried and longed for her with my whole heart. I had traveled 8,000 miles to rescue her from what could be a horrible life of poverty and hopelessness. And she rejected me. I was crushed.

I had to stop and wonder—what must God feel like when I do the same to Him? He sacrificed His beloved Son for me. He forgave me, loved me, cleaned me up, rescued me and adopted me. And I still choose to reject His plan for me so many times. I choose to turn my back and do it my own way.

The pain of my sin and rejection must hurt Him a million times more than what I experienced with Shas' rejection. And I was struck by the fact that even when I sin, He chooses to continue to love me unconditionally. During those first tumultuous days, I made a choice to love my daughter unconditionally. No matter how long it took, even if she never loved me, I would steadfastly give her my constant love and care. I am beyond thankful that although it was difficult, it was a relatively short amount of time before she chose to accept me.

In fact, Shas and Jarrott and I were chatting over lunch recently and she looked across the table at me and asked in her thick accent, "Did you always want an Indian princess with black hair and brown skin?"

"Yes, I did!" I assured her with a smile.

She thought about that for a moment and said, "I did not like you in India."

I laughed, "I know. But you like me now, huh?"

Her smile was huge. "Oh, yes, Mommy, I *love* you now."

And that made every moment of sacrifice, tears and rejection well worth the wait.

And it makes me wonder how great God feels when I finally get it right.

Well, Shas has fit right into our family. She and Jarrott are the best of friends and it is so great for him to have a little sister. He thoroughly enjoys teaching her new English words, helping her learn letters, and loves reading books to her. She is a priceless blessing to our family and I am grateful every day that God allowed our family, in a small way, to be the hands and feet of Christ to this precious little girl.

I don't know what new adventures God still has in store for the Millermon family, but I know wherever He leads us, He'll be there with us, every step of the way.

God's Mercy
By Paul Marino & Ginger Millermon © 2009

I found God's mercy
In an old wooden pew in 1983
When I realized He gave His life for me
He changed my heart
So unexpectedly
That's when I found God's mercy

I saw God's mercy
In a children's hospital room 223
My little boy was barely holding on to life
Then a miracle, it showed up one night
That's when I saw God's mercy

Oh, the Lord is so good
And His mercy is forever
And even if I could
Explain this mystery
How much He loves me
And it goes on and on
And on and on and on
And it goes on and on
And on and on and on

I held God's mercy
In an orphanage 8000 miles away
A little girl abandoned without hope
I promised her
I would take her home
That's when I held God's mercy
That's when I saw God's mercy
That's when I found God's mercy

188

Seeing Shasmita for the first time.

She loved looking in the mirror at her new clothes

Sova and Shas

Visiting the Taj Mahal

Discussion Questions for *Grace Thus Far:*

Dear reader,

Welcome to my discussion questions. I hope you're ready to dig deep and do some serious soul searching! For book clubs and discussion groups, if you're feeling adventurous, you can contact me at info@gingermillermon.com and I'd love to call in and answer any burning questions you might have during your discussion of *Grace Thus Far.*

Blessings!

Ginger

In-depth/Personal Questions:

1) What is the most difficult trial you've ever endured? How did you handle it? Tell about a time when you've seen God work a terrible situation for good in your life.

2) What are some Scripture verses that have been a particular comfort to you during trials you've endured?

3) Who are some Biblical characters whose lives have encouraged you in your trials? Why have their stories affected you?

4) Talk about a time in your life when you questioned God. When have you been angry and disappointed with Him? How did you resolve that anger—or do you still struggle, asking "why?"

5) If you've never been through a traumatic or tragic event in your life, how do you think you would handle it if you did? If you *have* been through tragedy, how do you wish you had handled it differently?

6) What is your worst fear? How do you deal with this fear?

7) Talk about losing someone you loved. Who was it? How did this death affect you?

8) Do you know someone with a special needs child? How does this affect the family dynamics?

9) In Chapter #10, I talk about having the "death of a dream" for Jarrott. Tell about a time you had to let go of an expectation or dream for your child.

10) Talk about a time that you experienced a long-term illness or long hospital stay with someone you love. How did you handle it? How did you grow, and what did you learn through it?

11) Tell about someone you've known or heard about who was given a poor medical prognosis and God miraculously turned the situation around. How did that affect your faith in God's abilities?

12) In Chapter #8, Joel and I had a care conference with Jarrott's doctors and they told us he was dying. God provided someone to bring us comfort in our tremendous grief that day. Tell about a time God provided someone to bring you comfort when you needed it most.

13) Have you ever been faced with the Sanctity of Human life issue? What are your thoughts on this cultural issue? What do you think God thinks about this issue? Do you know any Scripture that confirms your point of view?

14) Think about someone you know who is going through a terrible circumstance. How can you help? In what way can you practically show yourself to be a servant of Christ and show His love?

15) What are some unanswered questions in your life that are breaking your heart? Where will you go for help?

16) Talk about a time when you felt completely helpless in your circumstances. Did you rely on God's presence, or try to do it on your own?

17) In Chapter #7, my dad came to a place of realizing his need for God. When did you come to realize your need for a Savior? What questions do you still have about Christianity and a relationship with God?

18) Looking back over my teen years, I can see how God was preparing me for the intense trials I would experience in my twenties. As I mentioned in Chapter #5, I reached a place of hopelessness as a young teenager and tried to take my life. Instead of continuing to keep my desperation a secret, I went to my pastor and parents for help. I received the counseling and direction I needed and ultimately realized that God was enough for me, much like the story of Joseph. I believe that experience helped me later during our trials to be willing to swallow my pride and seek counseling for our hurting marriage.

What embarrassing or overwhelming problem in your life are you facing? Are you willing to push aside your pride and seek the help you need?

Other products available from Ginger Millermon:

"Rescued" CD © 2010 Anothen Music
Produced by Paul Marino.

"Beautiful Gift" CD © 2008 Anothen Music
Ginger's Christmas Album Produced by Paul Marino.
Also features a duet with McKenzie Millermon.

"Amazed" CD © 2007 Anothen Music
Produced by Paul Marino.
Includes 3 national Inspo "Top 10" singles.

"Picture of You" CD © 2004 Anothen Music
Ginger's 2004 project, which includes radio
"Top 40" songs *"I Lift Up My Eyes,"*
"All My Ways" & *"Fountain of Life"*
Produced by Jim Spencer.

"First Breath" CD © 2002
Ginger's debut album is a moving collection
of songs intended to direct your attention to
the transforming power of the cross and
all the riches that are ours in Christ Jesus.
Produced by Dan Smith.

For any of these products, please contact your local Christian bookstore
or visit Ginger's website at **www.gingermillermon.com**

Write a note to Ginger at:
    Ginger Millermon
    Anothen Music
    P.O. Box 624, Hutchinson, KS 67504
    info@gingermillermon.com

GINGER MILLERMON IS A nationally recognized women's conference speaker, author, songwriter, and recording artist, garnering multiple "Top 10" inspirational singles. She is in demand as a concert vocalist, women's speaker and worship leader. Her testimony and music has been featured on many national television and radio shows including the 700 Club and Focus on the Family.

Ginger lives with her family in the sand hills of Kansas.

To book Ginger for your conference, fundraiser or concert event, please contact her at info@gingermillermon.com or visit her website at www.gingermillermon.com

CPSIA information can be obtained at www.ICGtesting.com
Printed in the USA
BVOW03s1052201114

375903BV00007B/12/P